T0341421

ENTERPRISE

02.05

Angel Capital

William J. Bradley, Gerald A. Benjamin and Joel Margulis

- Fast track route to understanding the business of angel investing

- Covers the key areas of angel investing from understanding the inefficiencies of the marketplace and the evolution of the industry to developing a successful angel investing practice

- Examples and lessons from some of the world's most active private equity marketplaces, including the United States, Europe, Asia, the Middle East, and Australia

- Includes a glossary of key concepts and a comprehensive resources guide

>> EXPRESS EXEC.COM <<
essential management thinking at your fingertips

Copyright © Capstone Publishing 2002

The right of William J. Bradley, Gerald Benjamin and Joel Margulis to be identified as the authors of this work has been asserted in accordance with the Copyright, Designs and Patents Act 1988

First published 2002 by
Capstone Publishing (a Wiley company)
8 Newtec Place
Magdalen Road
Oxford OX4 1RE
United Kingdom
http://www.capstoneideas.com

CIP catalogue records for this book are available from the British Library and the US Library of Congress

ISBN 1-84112-235-1

This book is printed on acid-free paper

Substantial discounts on bulk quantities of Capstone books are available to corporations, professional associations and other organizations. Please contact Capstone for more details on +44 (0)1865 798 623 or (fax) +44 (0)1865 240 941 or (e-mail) info@wiley-capstone.co.uk

Contents

Introduction to ExpressExec

ExpressExec is 3 million words of the latest management thinking compiled into 10 modules. Each module contains 10 individual titles forming a comprehensive resource of current business practice written by leading practitioners in their field. From brand management to balanced scorecard, ExpressExec enables you to grasp the key concepts behind each subject and implement the theory immediately. Each of the 100 titles is available in print and electronic formats.

Through the ExpressExec.com Website you will discover that you can access the complete resource in a number of ways:

» printed books or e-books;
» e-content – PDF or XML (for licensed syndication) adding value to an intranet or Internet site;
» a corporate e-learning/knowledge management solution providing a cost-effective platform for developing skills and sharing knowledge within an organization;
» bespoke delivery – tailored solutions to solve your need.

Why not visit www.expressexec.com and register for free key management briefings, a monthly newsletter and interactive skills checklists. Share your ideas about ExpressExec and your thoughts about business today.

Please contact elound@wiley-capstone.co.uk for more information.

Introduction

This chapter introduces the concept of angel financing.

Angel investors are the single most significant source of growth capital on the globe. While the industry is often referred to as "hidden" or "invisible," make no mistake about it, a significant number of today's most significant companies were, at one time, the benefactors of angel capital.

The growing popularity of angel investing over time represents the greatest accumulation of wealth this planet has ever seen, having swelled the industry with more capital than at any other time in history. But while the growth of the industry is healthy, the number of new entrants incapable of making quality angel investment decisions is astounding.

The look of today's angel investor is much different from what it was just five years ago. Once, angel investors were, like their venture capital brethren, private equity investors involved in their investments. But many of today's newest angels seek a more passive approach toward their portfolio companies. While they remain interested in capturing the multiple returns promised by the asset class, they are not interested in nurturing that asset to harvest. The consequence is a growing number of failing angel-backed companies.

However, today's amateur angel investors may be facing unnecessary challenges. The needs of today's private market individual investors have spawned a growing number of quality service providers and angel organizations. While these organizations may provide little value to the purist, they offer excellent options for the market's newest entrants. Further, these organizations make for a more efficient angel marketplace.

Angel Capital was written to provide angel investors with a better understanding of the options available to them in today's marketplace. More opportunities are available to today's private market investors than at any time in the industry's history. *Angel Capital* is an excellent source of information for aspiring amateur angels, experienced professional angels, and all those who serve or seek capital from high-net-worth individuals.

OVERVIEW OF CONTENTS

Angel Capital is divided into ten chapters, each focusing on different aspects of the angel capital marketplace.

After this introduction in the first chapter, Chapter 2 offers a general overview of the industry, and defines the terms used throughout the text.

Chapter 3, "Evolution," presents a comprehensive look at the history of private equity investing. This chapter addresses historical aspects of both the angel capital marketplace, as well as the institutional venture capital marketplace. The impact of the Internet on the angel capital marketplace is examined in Chapter 4, which also focuses on today's most significant players and the services they make available to angels.

The global implications of angel investing and the challenges of cross-border angel investing are outlined in Chapter 5. Chapter 6, "The State of the Art," focuses on today's marketplace, addressing the market's inefficiencies and examining the solutions.

Using case studies, Chapter 7 studies the private equity markets in the United States, Europe, Asia, Australia, the Middle East, and Latin America.

Chapter 8 consists of an A-Z glossary on the topic and Chapter 9 provides useful resources of practitioners, books, articles, Websites, etc.

The final chapter presents a step-by-step guide to angel capital investing, providing the reader with an excellent framework from which to build a customized methodology.

Angel Capital will help angel investors to develop a better understanding of their marketplace and provide a continuing source of useful information.

Definition of Terms

This chapter offers a general overview of the industry, and the terms used throughout the text.

This section of the book highlights some of the terminology used throughout the text. It provides the reader with a general overview of the industry and its players.

WHAT IS PRIVATE EQUITY INVESTING?

Private equity investing distinguishes itself from other types of investing by how intensely investors involve themselves in the investees' company. In contrast to passive public market investments, private equity investors are heavily involved in the on-going development of their private market portfolio companies.

Private equity investors often position themselves to more easily control the portfolio companies that receive their investment dollars. Investors often exercise control through their representation on the company's board of directors and/or through controlling ownership interest of the company itself. Because of the high risk associated with engaging virgin concepts, with talented, yet often inexperienced management teams, experienced private equity investors exercise a hands-on approach to managing their investments. The sector's success is defined by private equity investors' use of highly talented professionals to guide their start-up portfolio companies.

Private equity investors expend huge resources in managing and monitoring their portfolios. They absorb sizable expenses to chase abnormally high returns on their invested capital. These returns, however, do not come without risk. Private equity, as an asset class, tilts toward the highest end of the risk/reward curve. Private equity investors understand that the entire loss of capital in any one investment hovers as a possible outcome.

A further distinguishing characteristic of private equity is that private equity investments take place in the private capital markets, as opposed to the public markets. In the public markets, investors freely trade ownership stakes in companies daily on various exchanges, while in the private markets, those holding ownership stakes cannot trade freely.

Private equity investors include private equity firms, corporate or merchant banking divisions of large institutions, and angel investors.

THE ANGEL CAPITAL MARKET

The angel capital market consists of two types of players: angel investors and entrepreneurs.

Angels

The angel capital market is the largest source of capital for early-stage companies on the planet. "It is well documented in the United States and the UK that the business angel market is the largest source of risk financing for entrepreneurial firms, vastly exceeding the institutional venture capital industry." (Van Osnabrugge & Robinson) In fact, the National Venture Capital Association has suggested that the angel capital market may account for $100bn annually. (Van Osnabrugge & Robinson)

Angel investors are high-net-worth individuals who actively seek financial and hands-on involvement in early-stage companies. The angel investor is unique to the private capital markets in that angels typically provide capital where mainstream sources of capital are unavailable. That is, angels take the greatest capital risk of any private equity investors because they are often the first investors involved in early-stage companies.

An angel's ability to nurture the growth of his or her portfolio company is critical to the eventual success of the start-up. Angels are almost always veteran executives of industry who have ridden one or more companies to a successful harvesting event. As a result, angels generally focus their investments on those sectors where they have previously found success. By doing so, angels leverage their expertise to increase the chances of the start-up's success.

Angels, by nature, are very private individuals. Like the start-up companies they invest in, angels are stingy with information about themselves. The investment activity of angel investors is difficult to monitor because of:

» the very high number of transactions;
» the smaller and therefore less visible investments; and
» the high degree of confidentiality demanded by high-net-worth angels upon engagement.

The behind-scenes nature of angels contributes significantly to the inefficiencies of the marketplace.

Entrepreneurs

Start-up entrepreneurs are the target of angel investors endeavoring to capture the many rewards associated with uncovering the next groundbreaking idea or enterprise. As the initial financial backer, the angel captures not only a significant return on investment, but the personal satisfaction and social recognition associated with finding the next glittering vein of gold.

Angels typically target companies conceiving an idea, or financing research and development. The various stages of entrepreneurial development can be defined as:

» Seed: a venture in the idea stage or in the process of being organized.
» Research and development: financing of product development for early-stage or more developed companies.
» Start-up: a venture completing product development and initial marketing and has been in business less than two years.
» First stage: a venture with a working prototype that has gone through beta testing and is beginning commercialization.
» Expansion stage: a venture in the early stage of expanding commercialization and is in need of growth capital.
» Mezzanine: a venture that has increasing sales volume and is breaking even or is profitable. Additional funds are to be used for further expansion, marketing, or working capital.
» Bridge: a venture that requires short-term capital to reach a clearly defined and stable position.
» Acquisition/merger: a venture in need of capital to finance an acquisition or turnaround.
» Turnaround: a venture in need of capital to effect a change from un-profitability to profitability.

Source: *Angel Financing, How to Find and Invest in Private Equity*, Benjamin & Margulis, John Wiley & Sons, 2000.

Early-stage entrepreneurs face a significant challenge in capitalizing their initial development because their new company has little, if any, performance record. For example, the start-up company seeking

$100,000 of initial seed capital to finance the development of the business has limited options. Banks are unlikely to grant credit to seed-stage companies with a lack of history, and venture capitalists typically invest in companies seeking expansion funds in amounts much greater than that sought by the seed-stage entrepreneur.

While entrepreneurs may have outside avenues of capital, such as the "Small Business Administration," or friends, family, and founders, angels are the number one source of capital for start-ups.

VENTURE CAPITAL

Venture capital, like angel capital, finds its purpose in the financing of early-stage companies. Unlike angel capital, however, the venture capital marketplace is a highly institutionalized process, designed to bring together those with massive amounts of money to invest and those whose ideas are promising enough to warrant its receipt.

Venture capital firms are organizations designed to foster the institutional private equity process. The partners and professionals of these firms are typically high-achieving executives from an array of industries, including finance, technology, entrepreneurship, and legal/accounting. The industry prides itself on maintaining a high standard of membership.

Venture capital firms organize private equity funds, funds typically structured as limited partnerships in which the venture firm and/or its partners/subsidiary entities serve as the general partner, and institutions, such as pension funds, endowment funds, insurance companies, etc., serve as the limited partners. By and large, venture capital firms do not serve as sources of capital. While the firm may hold a minority position in each of its funds, the majority of capital that the fund manages comes from its institutional limited partners.

Like the entrepreneurs that they invest in, venture capital firms, before they commence operations, must capitalize themselves. To accomplish their goal, venture firms seek the risk capital investments of the world's largest corporate and government institutions. Venture capitalists present their value proposition to these institutions in an effort to gain commitments for the capitalization of their funds. Of note, venture firms allocate a minute percentage of their funds to high-net-worth individuals. However, venture firms do not typically solicit these individuals, but instead, offer participation to those who have existing relationships with the firm or its partners. Once institutional commitments have been received and a fund is capitalized, the firm is ready to manage its newly acquired investment dollars.

Venture capital funds typically invest in companies that have graduated the seed- and early-stage development and are looking for expansion capital for two reasons. First, by investing at later stages, there is less risk in the company and potentially less time to harvest. Second, the size of today's venture funds does not allow them to make smaller investments. Imagine a $1bn fund making a series of $100,000 investments. The firm would have to hire an army of people to manage the portfolio. Venture funds of today are looking for later-stage deals in which investment sizes are larger, risk is reduced, and the time frame to harvest is shrinking. Remember, venture funds are not investing their own capital; the reputations of those fund managers ride on their ability to kiss the right frogs.

RESOURCES

Angel Investing: Matching Start-up Funds with Start-Up Companies, 2000, Mark Van Osnabrugge, Robert J. Robinson, Jossey-Bass, Inc.
Angel Financing, How to Find and Invest in Private Equity, 2000, Benjamin & Margulis, John Wiley & Sons.

Evolution

This chapter presents a comprehensive look at the history of private equity investing. This chapter addresses historical aspects of both the angel capital marketplace, as well as the institutional, venture capital marketplace.

The history of angel investing is, at best, poorly documented. Consider that even with today's advanced information-gathering capabilities, angel activity is not, and cannot realistically be, formally tracked. The gross number of angel transactions, the concealed nature of angels, and the relatively small investment sizes – all contribute to the difficulty behind building a formal picture of the marketplace, historical or otherwise. As such, and appropriately, an evolutionary look at the private equity market requires an examination of the history of angel investing, as well as of institutional venture capital.

A BRIEF HISTORY OF ANGEL INVESTING

In the 1920s and 30s, the term "angel investor" was the nomenclature used to describe individuals or wealthy families who, because of their belief in the importance of culture and entertainment in the time of economic turmoil, helped finance Broadway shows. But although the terminology may not have existed prior to 1920s and 30s, angels were active up to thousands of years before their Broadway followers.

Ancient Greek dramas were staged thanks to some of the polis's wealthy patrons. In 1492, Christopher Columbus capitalized his venture to the New World with "angel" funds obtained from Ferdinand and Isabella of Spain (Levin). In 1874, Alexander Graham Bell seeded Bell Telephone, and in 1903 five angels invested $40,000 into Henry's Ford's venture (Osnabrugge & Robinson). Changes have been the norm since the launch of Bell Telephone, not the least of which is the investment focus of the angel investor.

It was not until roughly 30 years ago that the angel investor re-gained the limelight as the premier financier of seed-stage business ventures. As such, angel investors have been the impetus behind some of the most famous companies in the world. Arthur Rock, one of the most famous and successful angel investors in history, helped to fund the early development of many of the more notable high tech companies, not the least of which was Apple Computer. Rock's $1.5mn infusion into Apple in the early 80s netted him a savory $100mn. Angels like Rock have always been recognized as savior figures, providing not only capital to capital hungry ventures, but some level of expertise.

Angel investor success stories like those of Arthur Rock demonstrate the impact angel investing has had not only on early-stage companies but perhaps more significantly, on the global advancement of technology through entrepreneurship. While the general purpose and concept of angel investing has remained constant over time, the ever-expanding size of the angel market has engendered a new breed of angel.

As high-net-worth individuals, angels have not always been the easiest target for entrepreneurs. Successful angels are known for their ability to remain "plugged in," while comfortably holding their ground behind the scenes. The recent popularity of angel investing has made angels more accessible than ever to the entrepreneurial public. In the days before angel clubs or online matchmaking environments, angels were much more difficult to locate.

Angel investors have typically been viewed as individuals capable of not only financial contribution to an emerging venture, but, perhaps as important, managerial and strategic contribution. The popularity of angel investing in the greater media has led to a significant increase in the number of high-net-worth individuals seeking private market investment opportunities. As such, a flood of new, inexperienced angel investors have emerged.

In many cases, today's inexperienced new breed of angel seeks the upside associated with traditional angel investing but often has little desire to contribute to the development of the venture beyond the original capital contribution. Enter the "passive" angel investor. While the general purpose remains the same – to seed emerging companies – the risk increases to both the entrepreneur and investor as the less-willing angel contributes little non-monetarily to the success of the venture.

The angel marketplace is being forced to evolve as more and more high-net-worth individuals participate. The structure of the market is changing to adapt to both the new passive nature of inexperienced angels as well as to the increased demands of the traditional investor. Nonetheless, the angel investor remains a staple in the emergence of start-up companies.

A BRIEF HISTORY OF VENTURE CAPITAL

The history of American venture capital is very colored. Interspersed throughout the industry's short life are government actions undertaken to spearhead the nurturing of new and promising companies. While the industry has always been recognized as a "clubby group" or an "old boys' club," its face has changed significantly to reveal today a highly publicized, multi-billion dollar global force of economic change. A look at its brief history provides insight into some of the more powerful individuals and groups that planted the roots of institutional venture capital and insight into the structure that governs today's market.

The first brave step

Most experts agree that the first institutional effort toward investing risk capital in early-stage companies came through an entity known as American Research and Development, or ARD. ARD, founded under Massachusetts law on June 6, 1946, claimed a management team heavily weighted in executives, professors, and affiliates of Massachusetts Institute of Technology (MIT). ARD's founders, however, originated separately.

Through his affiliation with ARD, General Georges Doriot is generally recognized as the father of venture capital. In 1946, Doriot, a professor at the Harvard Business School and long-time advocate of emerging companies, established ARD, along with Ralph Flanders, the then president of the Federal Reserve Bank in Boston. They attempted to capture a portion of the tremendous amount of capital being held by some of the nation's largest fiduciaries (insurance companies, pension funds, endowments, etc.) and redirect it toward the growth of emerging technologies.

ARD initially set out to raise $5mn. As the first entity of its kind, ARD faced a difficult road to capitalization. The process eventually led to the successful retention of $3.5mn ($500,000 more than the targeted minimum) from the likes of John Hancock Mutual Life Insurance Company and MIT. ARD was off and running.

ARD's investment/monitoring process was far from streamlined at the outset, but by the end of 1947, it had invested in eight companies: six startups and two existing concerns. For Doriot and the rest of the management team, ARD was a part-time obligation. But, as one could expect, the task at hand required more than a part-time effort to mentor the company's portfolio. Accordingly, Doriot was forced to channel a decent percentage of his effort toward the development of ARD's stable of companies, a decision that eventually led to success. By 1951, ten ARD-backed companies were operating at a profit.

While ARD was charting success with its portfolio, the most significant event of its time took place 11 years following its inception. ARD made an investment of $77,000 in a Massachusetts mini-computer manufacturer named Digital Equipment Corporation, or DEC. The investment, earning ARD 77% of the company, turned out to be the poster child of venture capital investing and put substance to the reward portion of the risk/reward model. ARD's investment in DEC increased the value of its portfolio by more than 5000% by 1971.

The next wave

The Small Business Investment Company (SBIC) Act of 1958, promulgated by the Small Business Administration (SBA), set in motion a process by which government-approved investment companies could leverage capital with the United States government on a four-to-one basis. The government's effort to spur the development of early-stage, emerging-growth companies created opportunities financiers had never seen before.

Under the new Act, the SBA would regulate the flow of funds but would leave the investment decisions to the professionals administering the private investment companies. The low interest leveraging capabilities of the Act created a different kind of investment company from what had previously been witnessed with ARD. While ARD was a seed-/early-stage equity investor, SBICs of the time were more inclined to structure debt investments with later-stage companies to reduce the risk of defaulting on their own obligations to the government.

The SBIC program proved to be attractive. By the mid-1960s, nearly 700 SBICs existed and in aggregate represented the largest supply of private market risk capital. The boom of the initial public offering (IPO) market added to the excitement of the industry and SBICs were bigger than ever.

Not until late 1969, with the downturn of the public markets, did the venture capital industry as a whole, and specifically the highly leveraged SBICs, begin their shakeout. From 1969–77, the weakness of the IPO market, the oil embargo, and the general weakness of the emerging capital sector created the greatest lull the private sector had seen since its inception. As SBIC portfolio companies turned south, the debt servicing obligations of the government-backed investment companies posed an ominous conundrum to the industry niche. Allegations of misrepresentation and fraud gave the sector a black-eye. In 1978, SBICs represented only 21% of the available risk capital pool. It became clear that in a down market, leveraged risk capital vehicles were dangerous investment structures.

Government intervention

In 1978, the venture capital industry changed its face forever. The American government, recognizing the need to spur the development of young companies, made significant efforts to loosen the environment for the creators of early-stage investment vehicles. The most significant changes were as follows.

» The Revenue Act (1978): provided capital gains tax incentive for equity investments. Capital committed increased by $556mn from the previous year.
» ERISA's "prudent man" rule (1979): clarified investment guidelines for pension investors to allow for higher risk investments.
» The Small Business Investment Incentive Act (1980): redefined venture firms as business development companies, eliminating the need for registering as an investment advisor.
» ERISA's "safe harbor" regulation (1980): stated that venture managers would not be considered fiduciaries of plan assets.
» The Economic Recovery Tax Act (1981): lowered capital gains rate. Capital commitments doubled to $1.3bn in 1981.
» The Tax Reform Act (1986): reduced incentive for long-term capital gains.

Source: T.A. Soja and J.E. Reyes, *Investment Benchmarks: Venture Capital* (Needham, MA: Venture Economics, Inc. 1990), p. 202

The force of the new legislation had an immediate impact on the industry. *The Venture Capital Journal* reports that in 1979, $460mn was invested in 375 companies by approximately 225 venture firms. By 1987, approximately 700 venture firms invested $3.94bn in 1,729 companies.

The last decade

The early part of the 1990s saw the industry pull back from its peak in 1987. As more and more firms came on the scene, competition for deals increased. Beginning in 1996, little did they know the venture capital industry would see its most significant run in history. And by the year 2000, according to PricewaterhouseCoopers' "Money Tree Survey," approximately $65bn was invested into venture-backed companies, a 76% increase over the amount invested by venture capitalists in 1999. In addition, private equity firms raised more money in 2000 than in any previous year, raising approximately $76bn, compared to the $59.23bn raised in 1999.

Over the past 50 years, the venture capital industry has ignited the greatest capitalist society the world has ever known. Structures and legislation have evolved to further promote venture activity and with it a multi-billion dollar industry. As the world continues to evolve with more advanced technologies, one can be sure that new ideas will garner opportunities never seen, thanks to today's robust angel and venture capital marketplaces.

RESOURCES

Venture Capital at the Crossroads, 1992, William D. Bygrave and Jeffry A. Timmons, Harvard Business School Press.

Money Tree Report 4th Quarter 2000, June 2001, Price Waterhouse Coopers.

Structuring Venture Capital, Private Equity, and Entrepreneurial Transactions, 2000, Jack S. Levin, Kirkland & Ellis.

Angel Investing: Matching Start-up Funds With Start-up Companies, 2000, Mark Van Osnabrugge & Robert J. Robinson, Jossey-Bass, Inc.

Investment Benchmarks: Venture Capital, 1990, T.A. Soja and J.E. Reyes, Venture Economics Inc., Needham, MA, p. 202.

The E-Dimension of Private Market Finance

This chapter examines the impact of the Internet on the angel capital marketplace. This chapter focuses on today's most significant players and the services they make available to angels.

The Internet, to a degree, has proven itself a practicable means of matching buyers and sellers of computers, books, and automobiles. But what of its ability to match buyers and sellers of private companies? In other words, does the Internet provide the means by which high-net-worth individuals can be matched with quality entrepreneurial projects?

Consider that, based on a study conducted by W.J. Bradley Company, 80% of investors say they would fund more early-stage deals if they could find the right ones. The individual private market investor, or "angel" investor, often struggles to gain access to high quality entrepreneurial deal flow. Is the Internet the answer?

While several online "matchmaking" services have surfaced, few have demonstrated the quality that high-net-worth investors seek. As the following analysis shows, the online financing population has been narrowed down to a few performers. Furthermore, while the companies highlighted in this chapter have gained some early recognition and momentum, the viability of the e-commerce model, as it relates to private equity finance, remains in question.

A BRIEF HISTORY

The history of raising capital over the Internet, like the history of any online marketplace, is short. The first worthy entrant, Garage.com, made its highly public splash into the online marketplace in October 1998. With the explosion of private capital markets at the same time, Garage created a rush of copycat websites designed to marry entrepreneurs and investors. By claiming accredited investor status (as defined by the Securities and Exchange Commission, Regulation D, Rule 501), one can register as such on one of many websites which will subsequently allow the investor to download business plans and/or view private market investment opportunities via the Internet.

Although the history of online matching services has been brief, the first three years have been turbulent. Many start-up companies designed to match wealthy individuals with entrepreneurs have either been forced to scale back business plans, lay off workers, or have gone bankrupt. For example, GE Venturemine.com, a division of GE Capital, and one of the more visible ventures in the space, ceased its operations on January 12, 2001. Certainly, the recent downturn of the financial markets and the overall depressed state of the economy have contributed to the turbulence, but the question remains, is online venture finance a workable business model?

Although many companies in the online matchmaking space still "exist," two dominate the marketplace: Garage Technology Ventures and OffRoad Capital.

GARAGE TECHNOLOGY VENTURES (FORMERLY GARAGE.COM)

"I am now an evangelist for any technology: I evangelize venture capitalists to entrepreneurs and I evangelize entrepreneurs to venture capitalists."

Guy Kawasaki, founder, Garage Technology Ventures (Up Magazine, May 2001)

Founded in May 1998 by Guy Kawasaki, California based Garage Technology Ventures (Garage) invites angel investors, venture capital firms, and large corporations to become members of its online community. Garage's investor membership is comprised of 40% angel investors, 40% venture capital firms, and 20% corporate investors.

Investors

Garage's member investors must not only meet the SEC's accredited investor requirements to qualify, but also demonstrate the ability to add value to Garage's portfolio companies. Member investor fees, once $10,000 for institutional investors and $2000 for angel investors, have recently been waived. However, member institutional investors should hold minimum assets of $10mn, be able to make a minimum investment of $250,000, have a minimum *liquid* net worth of $1mn, and be able to make a minimum investment of $50,000.

Garage posits that one of the many benefits of investor membership is the quality of its deal flow. In fact, on average, Garage posts only one of every one hundred entrepreneur applicants for investor viewing on its website. Following the completion of an investor profile, member investors are either e-mailed or faxed (based on preference) deal flow that matches their criteria as set forth in the investor profile. Once the member investor identifies an opportunity of interest, the member investor's profile, at their election, will be released to the portfolio company. Further involvement is at the discretion of the portfolio company.

Entrepreneurs

Entrepreneurial applicants fill out a company overview that Garage's evaluation team reviews. Should the evaluation team determine that the applicant's project may be of interest to its member investors, Garage sets up a face-to-face meeting. Following an entrepreneur presentation, Garage determines whether to invite the entrepreneur to become a Garage portfolio company. Garage bases its approval on four factors:

1 Sector: companies in large, emerging technology sectors.
2 Stage: early-stage companies that seek a first or second round of financing of between $2mn and $10mn.
3 Growth: companies that demonstrate the ability to capture market share.
4 Team: companies with talented, seasoned entrepreneurs.

Revenue model

Garage's revenue model is cash and equity based. Garage earns a placement fee should a portfolio company find financing and retains the opportunity to purchase stock in the entrepreneur as it works its way through the Garage process.

Track record

Since its inception, Garage has arranged an impressive 77 transactions, raising more than $285mn in equity financing for early-stage technology companies. Further, Garage recently partnered with CalPERS (California Public Employees Retirement System) to form the Garage California Entrepreneurs Fund, a $10mn venture fund in which CalPERS is the exclusive limited partner, in addition to closing Garage Investments II, LP in which 3i (a leading international venture firm) is the exclusive limited partner.

Garage has attracted the deserved respect of top industry players and boasts an enviable investor base which includes Compaq chairman Ben Rosen and Robertson Stephens founder Sandy Robertson. Although Garage pulled its IPO bid in October of 2000 the company certainly looks likely to last.

OFFROAD CAPITAL

"It's a great concept," says Bill Burnham, general partner at Softbank Capital Partners . . .

"It would be pretty hard to aggregate all those people another way. The broad reach of the OffRoad shows . . . also ensures better quality control, since SEC staffers might be among those watching."

Business 2.0, October 1999

OffRoad Capital (OffRoad) is a California based investment bank founded in May 1999 by former Intuit executive Stephen Pelletier. OffRoad Capital acts as an online private securities marketplace giving high-net-worth investors, advisors, and institutional investors access to private equity funds and private offerings of early-stage technology companies.

Investors

OffRoad investor clients register online through an application process that requires members to open a securities account with the OffRoad broker/dealer arm. With significant SEC influence on both the management team and the advisory board, investors can rest assured that every registration step they take will follow the letter of securities law. Investors must qualify as accredited investors (according to SEC guidelines), and expect to make investments of no less than $25,000. Membership fees are limited to a $250 annual renewal fee. OffRoad's one time $1000 initiation fee was recently waived.

Once admitted, investors receive OffRoad's meticulously screened investment opportunities either through e-mail on OffRoad investor's homepage (established upon member acceptance). Each offering is covered in accordance with OffRoad's commitment to full disclosure. OffRoad investors are given the opportunity to view online presentations, network among one another through an online investor forum, and direct any unanswered questions online to OffRoad's member relations department.

OffRoad investors, following their due diligence, express interest in an offering through OffRoad's unique auction process. Investors submit orders indicating the dollar amount they want to invest and the per share price at which they would like to buy. Through its auction process, OffRoad creates an orderly marketplace where private securities are aptly priced. In the end, every investor pays the same share price, which may or may not be the same as the original offering price set according to an independent valuation performed by OffRoad prior to posting.

Following their investments, OffRoad investors benefit through the company's unique "reporting" requirements. Companies or private equity funds capitalized through OffRoad are required to report performance quarterly and annually to the OffRoad investor community. The reporting system, unknown to the private markets, brings to the private sector the disclosure of the public marketplace.

Entrepreneurs

OffRoad's entrepreneur process is representative of what a company going public might experience with its investment bank. The process is thorough in that OffRoad identifies, structures, values, and eventually places the opportunity.

In identifying investment opportunities, OffRoad seeks more established companies who have experienced a prior institutional round or have identified and secured a lead institution for the current round. In structuring and valuing an opportunity, OffRoad leverages not only their team, but a network of advisors to create a salable structure consistent with market prices. Through its "OffRoad Show" process, OffRoad provides its entrepreneurial clients with the opportunity to deliver multimedia presentations to the OffRoad investor base and network with OffRoad at the investor's discretion. OffRoad claims to close most transactions inside 90 days and states that only two of 15 deals have not been fully subscribed (*Bloomberg Wealth Manager*, February 2001, page 62).

Revenue model

Like Garage, OffRoad's revenue model is cash and equity based. Should a company find capital through the OffRoad process, OffRoad takes a cash fee equivalent to between 6% and 8% of the equity the company amasses. Further, OffRoad receives warrants worth between 1% and 2% of the company. (*Bloomberg Wealth Manager*, February 2001, page 62).

Track record

Since its inception, OffRoad has completed 14 private offerings of more than $100mn. In July 1999, OffRoad became the first organization to place private securities over the Internet. In February 2001, OffRoad completed the first online capitalization of a venture capital fund.

OffRoad Capital presents a unique value proposition to both investors and entrepreneurs. The company's technology platform, which successfully hosts OffRoad's proprietary online private securities marketplace, has led to unprecedented events in online finance. The financial community dare take notice.

LOOKING AHEAD

Can the Internet act as a practicable medium for the financing of early stage companies? The apparent success of companies like Garage Technology Ventures and OffRoad Capital provides hints that the industry is here to stay. However, ongoing success for Garage and OffRoad weighs heavily on the success of their respective portfolios. Should either company prove to be a catalyst to successful venture investing through the metrics of investment return, investors and entrepreneurs will flock. More investors, more deals, more opportunities. Should their portfolio companies flop, so goes their e-commerce model and, with it, their investor base.

Will other players surface leveraging the visibility of Garage and OffRoad? New players with any chance to succeed will likely surface as new ventures of established financial institutions. The days of the start-up online matchmaking extravaganza are probably over. Several quality middle tier players exist today whose long-term viability, like Garage or OffRoad will also rely on the success of their existing portfolio.

Perhaps as important as portfolio success will be their ability to create strategic partnerships, thereby strengthening deal flow, due diligence, and available capital.

Garage and OffRoad have proven that investors will invest in early-stage ventures presented online. As the marketplace matures, the face of online venture finance will inevitably evolve. Doubt remains whether the investor community will support an online marketplace in a slowing venture economy.

The Global Dimension

This chapter looks at the global implications of angel investing and outlines the challenges of cross-border angel investing.

Angel investing is a global activity. That is, angel investors exist in every emerging market across the globe. Angel investors, however, are not commonly cross border investors.

Angels tend to be "touchy-feely" with their private market investments. They like to be able, in theory, to reach out and touch their holdings. As such, most angel investments occur within a couple of hundred miles of the angel. The angel's close proximity to his or her private market investment portfolio eases monitoring responsibilities and promotes the value added aspects of the angel-entrepreneur relationship.

The globalization of the private equity market has an impact on the angel investor. With the emerging global marketplace comes the vitality and growth of the global private equity market – its opportunities for, as well as constraints on, angel investing.

THE TURN TOWARD GLOBALIZATION

Angel activity is tied directly to the institutional private equity marketplace. That is, where institutional private equity markets thrive, it is commonplace that a healthy seed stage, or angel capital market exists. Industry Standard's Tom Ehrenfeld states,

> "The surge in VC investment has only reinforced the importance of angel investing. As the stakes of venture capitalists increase, the importance of angels in nudging fledgling companies along is all the more critical."
>
> *The Industry Standard, June 2000*

Due to the lack of information available on global angel investing, we are forced to look toward the institutional global marketplace if we want to understand how globalization influences the global private equity markets.

Over the past few years, the private equity market in the United States has grown enormously. According to Venture Economics, the leading source for private equity statistics, the amount of capital raised by venture capital firms in 2000 was approximately $76bn, compared to $59.23bn raised in 1999. This astounding growth has attributed to success stories across the board not only for institutional private equity firms, but also entrepreneurs, and the angel investors who seeded them. But in April 2000, everything changed.

As the Internet "craze" fizzled, institutions were faced with countless issues. Private equity institutions watched portfolio companies lose as much as 90% of their value, and in certain cases saw investments wash completely off the books. Domestic pressures forced fiduciaries to turn to alternative, emerging markets for relief.

"These days, VC firms aren't just pitching their connections in Silicon Valley, Boston, or Austin. Although some of the losses were substantial, many firms generated huge profits during the boom. As a result, they see the same type of opportunities within foreign countries approaching the economic cycle the United States has already gone through. They are telling entrepreneurs what they can do for them in Hong Kong, Singapore and London."

> *The Industry Standard, Venture Buzz: When VC Firms Go Global by Vishesh Kumar, April 13, 2001.*

REASONING BEHIND GLOBALIZATION

According to Venture Economics and the National Venture Capital Association, US private equity investment in foreign companies soared from $1.1bn in 1997 to $7bn through the second quarter of 2000. Several factors contribute to the global institutional growth: the global adoption of technology, the size of emerging markets, and the loosening of once restrictive growth policies.

"The high adoption rates of Internet and wireless technologies abroad and a burgeoning entrepreneurialism around the world have made foreign private investment more attractive than ever."

> *The Industry Standard, Global Funding by Lark Park, November 20, 2000.*

The rush toward global entrepreneurialism is naturally courted by an increased demand in capital. With this in mind, large private equity firms have moved overseas to take advantage of the plethora of valuable investment opportunities in burgeoning entrepreneurial economies.

The sheer size of the global emerging economy, from a population perspective (read customer base), makes it a prime target for growth capital.

"With only five per cent of the world's population inhabiting the US, the populations of Europe, Asia, Africa, and Latin America contain large and growing segments of affluence for which the technology fields have great attraction."
Venture Capital Journal, Viewpoint: Partnering Advice for Successful Overseas Ventures by Jonathan Bell, July 1, 2000.

When the government softened regulations about investing abroad, investors found investing in foreign economies less cumbersome. Recently, several countries have shifted from a regulated economy to a free market, offering tax incentives and making available limited liability structures to reduce risk and spur growth.

Facts and figures

While several things have contributed to more capital available worldwide – the state of the US economy, the value proposition of emerging, highly populated economies, and loosening government regulations – the truth is that a number of private equity institutions have for years exercised a global presence. Driven by investment focus, opportunity, or the need to place capital, private capital is no stranger in a strange land. Whatever the reasons, the growing amount of available capital is astounding.

Recent examples of global funds being raised: Whitney & Co. currently capitalizing a $2bn global fund; Softbank earmarking $2bn for investments outside of the US and Japan; and Draper Fisher Jurvetson reportedly raising a $1bn global fund called ePlanet. In addition, Walden International recently raising a $1bn global fund expected to make significant investments in Asia, and Benchmark Capital closing a $750mn European fund in May of 2000 (Lark Park). While the numbers are impressive, they provide only a glimpse of the total picture, a mere indication of what is to follow.

THE GLOBAL ANGEL?

As private equity continues to grow within foreign jurisdictions, the growth of the local angel market is soon to follow. While angel investment contributes significantly to the growth of any emerging market, it is institutional capital that carries ventures to harvest.

As private capital floods emerging markets, and liquidity events occur, angels, albeit behind the scenes, are experiencing greater wealth. Angel success leads to more angel investment dollars not only by repeat angel investors, but by new entrants who seek to duplicate the success of their predecessors. The emerging market process is truly cyclical: angels seed the growth of the economy, which subsequently attracts institutional interest, which in turn spurs the local angel economy, which then seeds additional growth, and so on.

As private equity markets grow, and institutional investors create more opportunities by increasing the chances of liquidation of private market investments, the individual angel investor faces new challenges beyond those faced domestically.

While angel capital is a global marketplace, angel investors are not global investors. That is, as angel investing is burgeoning around the globe, the average angel investor is still struggling to figure out the domestic puzzle. The road to successful angel investing is sophisticated. The challenges of creating deal flow, evaluating investment opportunities, and monitoring investments to harvest have proved significant for angel investors. As angels look abroad to burgeoning markets and read about the plethora of investment opportunities and values, interest is certain to be peaked. As such, a new set of challenges surface.

Obvious challenges to foreign investing include the language barrier, time zone differences, currency variations, unfamiliar business practices, government laws and regulations, and, of course, geographic barriers. The recent global events surrounding the fight against terrorism only add to the existing difficulties of cross-border private investing. Angels must confront these challenges with any foreign investments.

The private market is an information problematic market. That is, gathering information on small, early-stage companies can often be difficult. We find little information on the new technology; the principals have no history; the market is underdeveloped, and so on. As one ventures onto foreign soil, he or she tackles still more sophisticated challenges. Not only must the angel deal with the standard challenges of foreign investment noted above, information gathering is woven into the mix to present a most difficult proposition.

Are there immediate solutions to the issues? Not necessarily. Formalized angel investing is a relatively new market. Institutional investors take advantage of foreign opportunities by opening offices abroad and staffing them with talented executives. This foreign presence provides the institution with the ability to properly identify, evaluate, and monitor private market investments. The angel does not have this luxury.

IDENTIFYING GLOBAL INVESTMENT OPPORTUNITIES

Sometimes angel investors struggle to tap into quality deal flow sources within their own region. Magnify that struggle significantly, and you have a clear picture of what an angel might face looking to identify foreign ventures of quality.

Angel investing is predominantly a local practice. While the opportunity to connect within foreign boundaries exists, it is not easy. Imagine, for example, trying to develop a network of attorneys, accountants, government contacts, and other angels in another country. For the average angel, the task is nearly insurmountable.

Unless an angel is willing to travel often, he or she will meet headlong the on-going challenge of identifying global opportunities. For any angel seeking overseas involvement, tapping into a quality foreign network for deal flow, expertise, and information becomes a must.

Another important issue an angel faces when considering foreign involvement is that the foreign entrepreneur may be unwilling to deal with an absent angel investor who probably has little influence in the entrepreneur's locale. That is, the entrepreneur will question the true value added by a foreign angel investor to a domestic venture. Angels will be not only challenged to identify quality foreign ventures but will face discrimination with respect to their ability to be actively involved in the strategic development of the ventures they seek to invest in.

EVALUATING GLOBAL INVESTMENT OPPORTUNITIES

Angels who evaluate domestic investments require in-depth knowledge of the market, access to information and expertise, and a thorough understanding of the entrepreneur's value proposition. As previously mentioned, every private market investor faces the information problematic issues surrounding private market investments in general. The proper evaluation of foreign market opportunities requires angels to establish a network to bridge the gap between the information necessary to conduct due diligence, and that provided by the capital seeking entrepreneur. The angel's ability to evaluate and select quality foreign investment opportunities becomes severely limited by the absence of an information channel.

Furthermore, foreign currencies, markets, valuations, customary business practices, government implications – all are different from their domestic counterparts. Acquiring knowledge of how to conduct business abroad should be the first step in making the leap across the border.

MONITORING GLOBAL INVESTMENTS

Properly monitoring private market investments requires that an angel be not only present, but prepared to provide assistance to the venture as it requires guidance through its growth stages. The most valued (and sought after) angels are those who not only provide the guidance needed, but create opportunities not ordinarily available to the entrepreneur. When an angel is plugged into a foreign economy, he or she is rarely able to add true value to the venture.

Monitoring can be a full-time job. Interactive monitoring of an overseas venture is, for most angels, nearly impossible. More often than not, should an angel be able to identify and properly evaluate a foreign venture, his or her monitoring capability is often passive, or facilitated through a foreign fiduciary. Further, the global fight against terrorism has direct implications on angels' ability to monitor foreign investments as a result of the heightened constraints on travel.

ANGEL IMPLICATIONS: LOOKING AHEAD

As borders lift, communication unifies, and information flows more freely, foreign opportunities may become more plausible for angel investors. The market is simply too localized today to cross international borders.

The presence of formalized networks across states and borders may curb the current local focus of angels by leveraging the power of the network. Unfortunately, very few national or international angel networks exist today. As more international opportunities arise the arrival of quality international angel networks is certain to follow.

REFERENCES

The Industry Standard, June 19, 2000, "Book Review: Angel Investing: Matching Startup Funds With Startup Companies," Tom Ehrenfeld.

Private Equity Week, May 2, 2001, "First Quarter VC Disbursements Take A Dive," Dan Primack.

The Industry Standard, April 13, 2001, "Venture Buzz: When VC Firms Go Global," Vishesh Kumar.

The Industry Standard, November 20, 2000, "Global Funding," Lark Park.

Venture Capital Journal, July 1, 2000, "Viewpoint: Partnering Advice for Successful Overseas Ventures," Jonathan Bell.

The State of the Art

This chapter studies today's marketplace. This chapter addresses the market's inefficiencies and outlines the solutions.

THE MARKET

"Angel investors have been referred to as the 'invisible' or 'hidden' market."

Gerald Benjamin

Depending on the source, the total number of angel investors in the United States ranges between 100,000 and 400,000. The low profile kept by angels contributes to the variance in the estimated size of the market. Angel investors, by nature, generally prefer to work "behind the scenes." In addition, tracking angel investments can be cumbersome; consider the number of $50, 000 − $100, 000 investments in entrepreneurial ventures that take place every day. Unlike the multi-million dollar institutional transactions, the relatively small angel transactions are often not followed by the greater media or reported to the companies that track the private equity industry. The "hidden" nature of the angel, combined with the challenge of tracking every angel investment, makes pinpointing the exact size of the market nearly impossible.

The amounts of angel investments are estimated, in any given year, to be between one to two times the size of institutional venture output. In 1999, for example, a banner year for the private equity markets, angel investments were estimated to have reached nearly $100bn. The overall size of the investment base in number and in transaction amount makes angel investing one of the most underestimated financial treasures on the globe.

"For early-stage private companies experiencing sales under $5 million, serving non-global markets, seeking smaller rounds (typically $250,000 to $1,500,000), lacking patented technologies, and resting among industries not currently the rage of Wall Street, Sand Hill Road, and Route 128, angel investors remain the primary source of funding for early- and expansion-stage capital."

Angel Financing, How to Find and Invest in Private Equity,
Gerald A. Benjamin and Joel B. Margulis, 2000

Today, angel investors represent the largest global source of seed-stage risk capital. While institutional private equity investors once boasted likewise, today's institutional private equity fund has grown beyond the scope of the seed market. That is, as venture funds continue to grow into the billions of dollars, the average institutional investment continues to increase. Today's venture firms are concluding larger and larger deals. As such, the need for the angel investor is now greater than ever. Not only are angels in demand by seed-stage entrepreneurs, but the venture firms who are financing second and third rounds are relying on the angels to increase the pipeline of quality deal flow.

> "[T]he surge in VC investment has only reinforced the importance of angel investing. As the stakes of venture capitalists increase, the importance of angels in nudging fledgling companies along is all the more critical."
> *The Industry Standard, Ehrenfeld, June 19, 2000*

The relatively recent widespread awareness of angel investing has developed it into a formal marketplace. Institutional venture capital, through its evolvement from a once clubby, tight-knit community to a global market, has paved the road to a more sophisticated, expanded view of the private equity market. As more and more high-net-worth individuals catch scent of the trendy angel marketplace and its many noted opportunities, the number of active angel investors grows.

But with the growth and popularity of the market has come a sea of less-experienced angel investors. The market is awash in angel investors more apt to stumble and make poor private market investment decisions. When these less-experienced investors make increasing numbers of bad decisions, we need to examine in more detail the inefficiencies of the current market structure.

INEFFICIENCIES

Why is it that angel investors typically show rates of return that, on average, fall below those of their VC brethren? The discrepancy exists because the angel investor market is fragmented, lacks the structured efficiency and sophistication of the institutional marketplace, and, most importantly, consists largely of non-professional investors. Most angels do not have the time to identify, evaluate, and monitor early-stage companies, while venture capitalists are professional investors who do just that.

The angel capital market is littered with inefficiencies. Angels struggle to create quality deal flow, to conduct proper due diligence, to properly negotiate investment terms, and to monitor their own investments. Further, as the market structure has flattened, and as angels have accrued more money, they have made an astounding number of poor investments. The overall lack of structure in recent years, as more money has become available to angels, has contributed to the number of poor angel investments. The unsophisticated angel has proven to be easy prey for the savvy entrepreneur. So, let us take a closer look at inefficiencies of the marketplace.

Deal flow

The majority of angel investors struggle to create quality deal flow. Deal flow is not difficult to create with a proactive approach toward its generation. That is, most any individual with money to spend can talk his way into deal flow with little effort. However, generating quality deal flow by getting plugged into the right networks is another story altogether.

Angel capitalized entrepreneurial ventures that fail are ultimately those that have difficulty finding follow-on financing beyond the initial angel round. These ventures bleed to death either because they are not worthy of institutional follow-on financing, or because the principals and current investors lack the network necessary to connect the project to its next round of funding. Angel capitalized entrepreneurial ventures that succeed are those that capitalize themselves to a liquidity event. In an angel capitalized venture, the source of the deal can make the difference between the angel who finds follow-on financing and the angel who doesn't.

Too often angels rely on a limited supply of deals or a poorly developed network to assemble their private market investment opportunities. Inexperienced angels will often fall prey to the "can't say no" syndrome, ending up with positions in low-quality deals that have little or no chance of eventual success.

Angels plugged in to their regional venture community are likely to see the highest quality deal flow. Venture opportunities that present themselves to angels through sophisticated networks that include venture capitalists, investment banks, top tier law and accounting firms, or other high profile angels, are often those ventures that, because of their source, have the greatest chance of success for follow-on financing. Further, angels who involve themselves in top quality referral networks will recognize that the quality of deals available – setting aside their increased chance of follow-on financing resulting from the source – far surpasses that of deals sourced through family and friends or poorly developed referral networks.

Due diligence

Due diligence comes in many flavors. We don't know of any universally accepted method of conducting due diligence, but any method should cover certain bases. Yet few angels understand what those bases are, and so make ill-advised investment decisions. For example, few angel investors appreciate the expertise, time and money that proper due diligence demands.

Proper due diligence, alone, requires access to experts who can assess the investment opportunity. To properly assess the investment opportunity, the angel needs access to experts with experience in the various sectors of the venture. In each venture, angels need experts in finance, technology, and industry to better understand the vastness of the opportunity – an understanding that far exceeds their own expertise.

Because the majority of angel investors are not professional investors, they find it difficult to carve out of their already crushing schedules time to conduct proper due diligence. Angel efforts at due diligence often fall short simply because the angel tires of making time to spend researching investment opportunities and, therefore, becomes more willing to accept the opinions of others.

Covering all of the bases of due diligence can be very expensive. Outsourcing expertise, particularly quality expertise, is costly. Retaining accountants, attorneys, industry experts, and conducting background checks on the venture's principals, all contribute to a hefty bill. While worth every penny in the end, and highly advised, conducting proper due diligence will take its toll on the angel's pocketbook.

Negotiating

Negotiating private market investment terms is as much an art as it is a skill. Keeping up with and possessing knowledge of the ever-evolving number of investment structures and their hybrids, are tasks unto themselves.

Many angels don't understand private market investment terms. As such, an angel accepts the entrepreneur's proposed terms on the structure of the investment because the angel lacks the knowledge to counter the offer or to even recognize that the offer should be countered. So angels need professional help by an accountant, attorney, investment bank, or angel service provider to incorporate the proper investment structure. Appropriate structures should always protect the angel as much as possible while at the same time properly compensating the investors for their investment risks.

Monitoring

Monitoring private market investments can be a full-time job. Start-up and early-stage companies require hand-holding and guidance as they grow. Most angels lack either the time or expertise necessary to monitor their private market investments properly.

Early-stage companies often seek strategic angel investors. Of greatest value to the emerging entrepreneur is the angel who can create business opportunities *after* the investment. Unfortunately, most angels make passive investments, investments in which the angel prefers little or no involvement in the venture. When an angel chooses not to participate, the investment is more likely to fail. As such, experienced angels often position themselves in investments so they can contribute to the strategic needs of the venture.

STRUCTURE OF THE MARKET

At some point, inefficiency in any market is bound to demand structure. The angel marketplace has seen several attempts at structure in recent years as the popularity of angel investing has ballooned. Today's angel marketplace is generally structured into four factions:

1 lone angel investors
2 small, private groups of angels

3 formalized angel clubs
4 angel intermediary groups.

Lone angels

Certain angels are lone angels by choice and others by naiveté. Lone angels, at least those by self-admission, are often the most sophisticated breed of angel, possessing traits more common of the professional venture, or institutional investor. Lone angels, by naiveté, simply lack the network necessary to get plugged into their local angel marketplace. Further discussion about the lone angel refers to those who are so by self-admission.

Usually, successful lone angels are plugged into sophisticated networks of high-end professionals, firms, government contacts, etc. These contacts are not only a source of deal flow, but are often co-investors in venture opportunities. The lone angel's network eases the due diligence process and provides access to more information and expertise. The successful lone angel networks superbly.

Lone angels are professional investors. They seek positions in companies in which they can step in, contribute, administer growth, and exit. Lone angels involve themselves as operators of a portfolio of companies. As such, they invest in ventures consistent with their background that require active involvement.

The lone angel's background, and likely tie to the venture's sector, sets the platform for successfully negotiating the terms of the investment. The lone angel benefits by understanding what the project needs, and by structuring it accordingly. Further, lone angels' monitoring capabilities are built-in through either executive or board involvement, and are eased by their knowledge of and connections in the industry.

While lone angels rely on a strong network for deal flow and expertise, they are self-sufficient. That is, their ability to gather, disseminate, and use information that complements their skill set, and, as such, allows them to remain stand-alone from a position of leverage.

Small, private angel groups

Many angels invest in private market ventures in connection with small, private groups of fellow angels. The group approach allows angels to diversify not only the responsibilities of due diligence and deal flow, but the risk of investment. The private angel group is a hybrid of the lone angel and the angel club.

The members of small angel groups are likely not professional investors. They are high-net-worth executives or former executives seeking passive involvement in private market opportunities. The group approach permits angels not only to spread responsibility, but to specialize in different areas of venture investing.

The successful, small, private angel group consists of individual angels from different walks of life. These groups consist of successful executives from the legal, accounting, technology, and financial sectors of industry that leverage one another for deal flow and increased expertise used in evaluating and mentoring deals.

The small, private group – different from the lone angel but consistent with the angel club – is dependent on the strength of the combined network of the team. In many cases, the small, private angel group can be more successful than the larger angel club. The small group approach may increase the involvement of the individual members and be less cumbersome to deal with.

The small, private angel group is an excellent option for those angels who have neither the time nor the desire to act on a stand-alone basis, but who also reject the herd mentality of the larger angel club. Further, in many, less populated areas, the angel club may not be an option and the small, private group may offer the only opportunity to network private market opportunities. Regardless, the small, private angel group serves as an alternative to both the lone angel and angel club options.

Angel clubs

In recent years, more ambitious angels have gathered in a formal environment known as the "angel club." Angel clubs attempt to curb some of the inefficiencies of the marketplace. Though more than 150 angel clubs operate in the United States, they possess similar objectives: to isolate, finance, manage, and ultimately profit from entrepreneurial ventures.

Angel clubs subscribe to the theory that the whole is greater than the sum of the parts. Angel clubs operate locally. Members rank among the high-net-worth, high profile business people of the region. The group usually meets once per month over cocktails and the infamous "rubber chicken" dinner.

At each meeting, three to five entrepreneurs are invited to present deals, deals commonly sourced by incumbent members of the club who "sponsor" presenting entrepreneurs. Fellow members "rely" on the sponsoring member for the initial screening. Sponsoring members make every effort to insure the sponsored entrepreneur is qualified to avoid any embarrassment in front of the club. Further involvement and due diligence with respect to any venture is undertaken on a voluntary basis by interested members.

Angel clubs create a team atmosphere and allow angels to leverage the expertise of their fellow members. Depending on the quality of the membership, angel clubs can be very successful and active. According to one source, Silicon Valley Band of Angels

> "pours an average of $1.1 million a month into the (venture) market."
>
> *Angel Investor, September–October 2000*

While not every club is as prestigious or as active as the Band of Angels, the concept has caught on as more and more clubs surface globally.

The angel club has proven an alternative to lone or small group investing. The concept, while popular and successful in certain regions, does have its challenges in others. Whenever a large number of powerful people come together, particularly considering the leadership ability of the constituency, a struggle for hierarchy is bound to emerge. What often results is a follow-the-leader mentality that abandons the advantages of leveraging the experience of individual members. As a result, due diligence gets left in the hands of a few, and the quality of investments is more likely to suffer.

Angel clubs are organized as social events, and while they work hard to serve their purpose – assisting angel investors in funding early-stage ventures – their ability to prosper as organizations rests in the members' ability to orchestrate an orderly and efficient business environment.

Angel intermediary groups

Whenever a market segment experiences rapid growth, a slew of service providers are bound to follow. The angel community recognizes two types of service providers, or intermediaries, that provide services to both early stage entrepreneurs and angel investors:

» stand-alone finders
» boutique investment banks.

Stand-alone finder

In this market segment, quality is scarce, with more pretenders than players. Finders are often stand-alone executives or small groups of fewer than five executives. Finders are often veterans of the financial services industry, or are former successful entrepreneurs. In order for a finder to be successful, he or she must have not only quality deal flow, but a tight network of both angel investors and institutional venture capitalists. The quality of a finder's rolodex is testament to his or her success as a capital source.

Quality finders are skilled in identifying, evaluating, and presenting venture opportunities. Like successful angel investors (most finders are), quality finders are tied deeply to the regional investment community. Their network of affiliations includes the region's top legal, accounting, financial, and technological professionals. The finders' network serves not only as a source of deal flow, but as a plethora of information and expertise leveraged in the identification and evaluation of venture opportunities.

Before presenting any project to their prized investor network, finders make every effort to increase the quality of the venture. These efforts include refining the business plan and offering documents, refining financial statements and valuation propositions, and ensuring that the offering complies with all state and federal securities requirements. Further, the quality finder understands that the presentation of the offering materials is critical to soliciting interest and as such, works with the entrepreneur to perfect the presentation of the documents.

Once the offering package is in place, the finder works diligently with the entrepreneur on the proper methods of soliciting capital. They coach the entrepreneur in introductions, sales, and closing. Once the finder is comfortable with both the offering documents and the entrepreneur's ability to properly court its investors, the capital sourcing process begins.

The successful finder doesn't take long to generate interest in a venture. The quality finder's reputation precedes him or her, creating a highly receptive deal flow for the finder's investor network. Following the investor's receipt of the offering documents, the finder acts as a true intermediary in advancing the due diligence process of the entrepreneur's prospects by answering questions related to the venture and generally providing service as needed. Ultimately, should an investor prospect demonstrate interest, the finder facilitates interaction with the entrepreneur and positions the sale to be closed.

When fortunate entrepreneurs locate a quality finder willing to take their projects on, the prospects of obtaining financing increase significantly. Further, the value added by the finder through both the refinement of the offering documents as well as the coaching/mentoring aspect of the relationship, offer an invaluable service to the startup entrepreneur.

Quality finders also serve as an invaluable asset to their network of investors. Investors can count on not only quality deal flow, but also a proper set of offering documents, and a prepared entrepreneur. Further, the quality finder understands that its investor network is a golden egg and makes every effort to ensure that those ventures chosen for presentation are top quality, well structured, and properly priced. Because finders often take equity positions in their client entrepreneurs, through either fee or purchase, the finder also acts as an excellent monitor of investors' private market portfolios.

Fee structures for the stand-alone finder vary significantly, depending on experience, track record, licensing, and market conditions. Most top-tier finders require some level of retainer fee from the entrepreneur, due either up-front, or paid on a monthly basis over the term of the relationship. The finder is always compensated following the successful completion of the transaction. The fee is typically percentage driven, based on the size of transaction.

While finders present an excellent value proposition to both entrepreneurs and angel investors, at the highest level, they are very difficult to find. Both parties should conduct proper due diligence before any formal engagement is undertaken.

Boutique investment banks

One advantage of working with an investment bank is its licensed affiliation with the Securities and Exchange Commission and the National Association of Securities Dealers. Proper licensure provides for the examination of public disclosure documents related to the history of the firm and its principals, a valuable bit of information for any entrepreneur or angel investor.

Few top-tier investment banks interact with the angel marketplace. The transaction size ($250,000–$2,500,000) is simply too small to justify the resource commitment of the banks' high-priced labor. Smaller, regional investment banks ("boutiques") are more apt to entertain the idea of an angel stage placement should the opportunity lead to greater fees down the road.

Quality boutique banks, like quality finders, possess high-profile networks. Boutiques always have access to angel investors and will often provide them with a variety of services, in addition to sourcing them private market opportunities. The banks' local presence, in addition to its network, positions it to see a sizeable deal flow from which to draw its entrepreneurial clientele.

The boutique bank, like the quality finder, adds value to the capital-seeking entrepreneur. The entrepreneur works through the same venture refinement procedures as it does with the finder in his or her preparation for capital sourcing. In generating interest among its network of angel and institutional investors, the bank is more active in the solicitation process than is the finder. Further, the bank works its network of contacts to create not only funding but strategic partners, human capital, and further connections to the institutional financial community.

Because of its increased capacity, the boutique bank is positioned to take a more grandiose approach to the private placement process than the finder is. That is, the bank has access to greater amounts of capital through stronger networks of alternative capital sources and, commonly, through a broader base of angel investors. In fact, many boutiques will syndicate offerings through their own network of quality finders.

Like the finder, the investment bank earns retainer and "success" fees. Again, fees vary by deal size, region, track record, and the like.

A quality boutique shop remains an excellent resource for entrepreneurs and angel investors. Angels in a boutique network have access to some of the top-quality, early-stage deal flow in the region. While entrepreneurs will find the qualification process stringent, they can shift their gaze to a substantial upside.

A LOOK TO THE FUTURE – LIKELY TRENDS AND DEVELOPMENTS

As angel investing continues to gain popularity, more and more structure will develop to service its broader base. The most valuable services going forward will link angels to opportunities nationally and globally. Such networks will heal the inefficiencies of conducting angel investing cross borders and create private market opportunities angels have never seen before. While angel investing has gained wider acceptance globally, it remains an underdeveloped market. The greatest source of early-stage capital will not only get bigger, but, through its organization, get better.

Case Studies

This chapter looks at the private equity markets in the United States, Europe, Asia, Australia, the Middle East, and Latin America.

Venture capital is truly a global industry. While the United States is the dominant player worldwide, a number of countries claim blossoming private equity markets. *Industry Standard*'s Lark Park had this to say about global development outside the United States:

> "Europe is getting the lion's share of venture capital, with much of it going in to wireless and telecom deals. Asia follows with a mix of high-tech and low-tech deals. And behind Asia is Latin America, where companies are seeing more supply-chain and e-commerce investments."
>
> *The Industry Standard, Global Funding by Lark Park,*
> *November 20, 2000*

A closer look at the industry's globalization requires an examination of the following countries: the United States of America, Europe, Asia, Latin America, the Middle East, and Australia.

UNITED STATES OF AMERICA

An overview

The United States serves as the standard when it comes to venture capital investing. Venture capital's short history finds its formal institutional roots firmly planted in American soil. The American venture marketplace, year in and year out, raises more money in its venture funds than any other country on the globe. As such, American venture firms also disburse more money to early-stage companies than any other country worldwide. With the United States setting the pace for the rest of the world, all eyes are on the American market as it will not only have a significant impact on the rest of world, but, as a leading indicator, will provide invaluable insight into what global players can expect in their markets in years to come.

April 2000 is a significant date in American venture history. It has proven to be the hinge in what was, prior to April, the most significant growth period in the history of American venture capital. Since April, of course, the industry has been on a steady slide downward in light of a disappearing exit market for venture-backed companies.

The disappearance of a functioning exit market for early-stage companies finds its roots in a fledgling Internet economy. The new economy, spawned in the euphoric pre-April period, was highlighted by financings of unstable companies vowing to change forever the way business was conducted. The "dotcom" fallout, as the post-April period has been referred to, has led to the eventual decline of thousands of venture-backed companies, and with it, millions upon billions of venture investment dollars. As a result, the American venture landscape has been forever altered. And while the short-term effects appear to have had a detrimental impact on the industry, a healthier economy is likely to evolve.

The statistics

The year 2000 was a banner year for the American venture capital markets. While absolute numbers were greater than in any year previous, quarter upon quarter increases were declining, lending to the reality that the industry's growth period had peaked.

According to PricewaterhouseCoopers *Money Tree Survey*, approximately $65bn was invested into venture-backed companies in 2000, a 76% increase over the amount invested by venture capitalists in 1999. In addition, private equity firms raised more money in 2000 than in any previous year, raising approximately $76bn compared to the $59.23bn raised in 1999.

Examining recent 2001 data, second quarter 2001 equity investments into venture-backed companies fell to $8.2bn compared to $10.4bn in the first quarter 2001, a 21% decline but less than the 41% decline experienced from fourth quarter 2000 to first quarter 2001. Further, second quarter 2001 commitments to venture capital funds decreased 36% to $9.7bn from the first quarter's $15.1bn, and compared to second quarter 2000's $31bn, down 69%.

The National Venture Capital Association reports that while numbers are down

"the second quarter [2001] was still significant compared with commitment totals during the past decade and while 2001 is unlikely to eclipse totals of the prior two years, it is still on pace to receive the third-highest amount of capital raised since Venture Economics started tracking [the venture capital] market in 1969."

The cash crunch

The market's recent downturn has had a significant impact on the cash flow positions of America's early-stage companies. As a result, the country's start-up entrepreneurs have turned to their financial backers for support.

In an effort to salvage their investments, venture firms have been forced to re-focus. Instead of putting fund dollars toward new companies, venture firms have been forced to disburse existing firm funds into fledgling portfolio companies in an effort to bridge them to a liquidity event. With the fallout of the initial public market, and a mergers and acquisitions market that resembles a "red tag" sale more than anything else, masses of venture-backed companies are struggling to survive the quest. One significant problem exists: the financial backers of these cash starved orphans had not planned for such an event.

The result is that American fund managers, while reaching the bottom of their proverbial barrels to carry their portfolio the course, have been forced, in many cases, to raise what the industry terms "annex" funds. These funds are essentially "emergency" funds designed to support existing cash positions. Alan Salzman, managing partner with the San Bruno, California, based Vantage Point Venture Partners, explains the occurrence:

> "These VC firms didn't leave enough gas in the tank, that's essentially what happened. The environment has changed, and some of these firms got caught short. It happens."
>
> *VCJ, August 2001*

So while entrepreneurs tuck their tails between their legs and come begging to their financial backers for breathing room, their financial backers are essentially performing the same "dog-and-pony" show for their institutional limited partners.

Structuring changes

While American venture firms are struggling, they are not prostrating themselves. They are fighting back. The terms upon which these funds are willing to commit capital in today's tight market have become decidedly one-sided. Stephan Mallenbaum, a partner in the New York law offices of Jones, Day, Reavis, & Pogue, comments on the change:

"Nothing's normal today, but there was nothing normal about what was going on two or three years ago. People were writing checks because a company was in the right space or because everyone else was. Term sheets were easy – they were basically form sheets. Now they're intricate and tough deals."

VCJ, May 2001

More stringent terms and creative structuring highlight the steps taken to reduce the risks of investment. Carolina Braunschweig, senior editor of *Venture Capital Journal*, sums it up best:

"For start-ups capital is a lifeline. But in today's VC market, that lifeline now comes with a hefty price tag. Cash-strapped young companies currently raising capital are not only being forced to cede control of their enterprise, but they are also under pressure to agree to lower valuations and stringent terms."

VCJ, May 2001

Venture capitalists are employing fancy tactics, such as liquidation preferences, full-ratchet anti-dilution rights and participating convertible preferred stock to leverage their positions. The use of these provisions has created the most defensive private capital market the industry has seen in some time, if ever.

The exit market

Today's down market comes as a result of, more than anything else, a lackluster initial public offering market. Venture investors make money through the favorable exit of a portfolio company. The most favorable of all exits is the graduation of a privately held portfolio company to a public market in which a company's stock can be sold at multiples of the venture investor's purchase price. Unfortunately, for today's venture investors, initial public offerings have become extremely hard to come by. *Venture Capital Journal's* Carolina Braunschweig states:

"At the apex of the dotcom bubble, firms raised money to avoid missing the lucrative late-stage investments in advance of an IPO.

Now, however, the same firms are raising cash to support companies that can't go public."

According to *Venture Economics*, over the past five years, venture capitalists have invested $164.8bn in 8700 operating companies that are still privately held. *Venture Capital Journal* reports that:

"even in the wide-open financing environment of 1999, only 257 venture-backed companies went public and in 2000, that number fell to 232."

More dismally, only 11 companies went public in the first quarter of 2001 and September 2001 was the first month since April 1976 that no IPOs were offered. Dana Callow, managing general partner of Boston Millennia Partners, says:

"There's simply not enough capacity to get those companies out, which means your loss ratio goes higher."

Looking ahead

While the statistics point to a struggling initial public offering (IPO) market, and a venture capital market that appears to have reached a plateau, activity certainly has not dried up. The number of billion dollar venture funds has more than doubled over last year and while first-time funds struggle to get on the map, veterans of the industry continue to up their bids as they successfully launch second, third, and fourth funds.

Today's American venture capital market is different – it's more real, more grounded. It requires stronger business plans, more experienced management teams, and demonstrable customer bases. While the terms of investment are more stringent and exits harder to come by, the industry is adapting. Despite its trials and tribulations, the American venture capital market is relatively healthy and continues to set the standard for the world to follow.

EUROPE

"The [European] market is exploding. There has been a dramatic rise in Internet deals in Europe, particularly over the last six months because everybody sees the enormous wealth that has been created in the United States and thinks that Europe is next, and it probably is next."

Venture Capital Journal, European Internet Deals Soar Hoping to Replicate the Success of US Internet Deals, VCs Race to Back Hot Start-ups Across the Atlantic, editor Debra Lau, May 23, 2001

European venture capital, as early as seven years ago, was a relatively dormant asset class as a result of the lack of a true exit marketplace. The opportunity for private equity investors to exit, young, blossoming companies through the American style initial public offering (IPO) was non-existent. The sudden manifestation of an array of exchanges such as the London Stock Exchange's Alternative Investment Market, Paris based Nouveau Marche, German based Neuer Markt in Frankfurt, and Nasdaq Europe in Belgium provided immediate opportunities to an exit market once dominated by mergers and acquisitions.

While American involvement in European venture capital dates back approximately to the early 90s, the recent downturn in American markets has forced the country's top venture capital institutions to focus on alternative markets with exciting technology and value propositions. Several top-tier private equity firms have opened European offices in the last 24 months, including The Carlyle Group (Madrid), Vestar Capital Partners (Milan), General Atlantic Partners (Munich), Veronis Suhler percent Associates (London), The Blackstone Group (London), Clayton, Dubilier percent Rice (Frankfurt), Benchmark Capital (London), Summit Partners (London), Texas Pacific Group (London), and Draper Fisher Jurvetson (London). The increase in the number of players in Europe has contributed significantly to the amount of capital available for early stage companies.

The year 2000 proved to be a banner year for private equity in Europe. *Venture Economics* reports that a total of Euro 57bn was raised for private equity funds, a 128% increase over 1999. Further, the statistics show that Europe continues to be recognized as a fertile venture climate by non-European private equity players. The European

Venture Capital Association (EVCA) reports a 5% increase in funds raised from non-European countries, from 22% in 1999 to 27% in 2000, led by the United States.

Despite the documented growth in private equity funds available, Europe has not eluded the recent downturn experienced in the United States. First quarter 2001 figures demonstrate the trend. *Venture Economics* reports that European private equity investment fell 60% in Q1 2001 from the Q4 2000 period.

The European venture capital market is commonly recognized as lagging behind United States activity. The continued financing of European-based Internet-related companies in 2000 demonstrates the effect, considering the significant drop-off in the same sector financings of US-based companies over the same period. Venture investment into Internet-specific European companies rose an astonishing 300% from 1999–2000, while US-based same sector, same-period activity increased 89.5%. Further, in its *2000 Yearbook*, the European Venture Capital Association reported that the combined high-tech sectors made up 31% of all capital distributions in 2000, up 26% from 1999. Taking advantage of the opportunity, US-based venture capital firms committed an eye-opening 56% of total capital invested in 2000.

Private equity investment across Europe does not represent an even distribution. The accelerated development of the Internet in Western European countries relative to non-Western regions of the continent contribute significantly to the uneven distribution of private equity dollars.

"[Non-Western] parts of Europe are behind when it comes to the Internet, but I don't think you'll see the types of investment in Central Europe into Internet companies like you saw in Western Europe or, especially in the US," says Gyuri Karady, who runs a central European fund for Baring Private Equity. "The risk has just proven to be too great."

The amount of capital flowing into private equity funds in 2000 by country, supports Karady's claim: United Kingdom (40%), France (22%), Italy (17%), Germany (9%), Sweden (4%), Finland (3%), Netherlands (3%), Switzerland (1%), Denmark (1%), Spain (1%).

Europe continues to foster its private equity growth through country-specific reforms designed to cater to greater venture investment opportunities. Adre Jaeggi, managing director of Adveq Management, Zurich/Switzerland, states:

> "The German tax reform, which took effect in 2001 definitely unlocks new buyout opportunities. Spain has already decided on a very similar tax reform. France has announced an overhaul of its fiscal regime over the next three years."

Further, recent tax initiatives in the United Kingdom further the cause.

ASIA

Japan

Japan is a blossoming private equity marketplace. Despite the fact that the Japanese economy is riding a rough tide, venture capitalists see the world's second largest economy as an "underdeveloped Silicon Valley" (*VCJ*, January 2001). As such, many top-tier venture firms, including American-based venture firms, are focused on Japan in an effort to capitalize on the potential growth opportunity.

In May 2001, Japan's minister of economics, trade and industry, Takeo Hiranuma, proposed a plan to create 1000 venture firms over a three-year period. Considering Japan's venture history, Mr. Hiranuma's goals are aggressive.

Before 1995, Japan's regulatory structure made it difficult for venture capital to exist, let alone prosper. As Yoshito Hori, chairman and chief executive officer of Apax Globis Partners percent Company, states:

> "Before 1995, VC's were not allowed to sit on the board of portfolio companies, limited partnerships were not allowed, pension funds were not allowed to invest into venture capital funds, and there were no stock options allowed."
>
> *VCJ, September 2001*

Since 1995, several deregulatory actions have been taken to loosen the industry. The creation of the Limited Partnership Act, the Jasdaq and Mothers (or Market of the High-growth and Emerging Stocks), and the introduction of stock options have all served to spawn a growing private equity market. Further, the ministry of international trade and investment (MITI) created a division to promote venture capital, providing grants of up to $500,000 for start-up companies.

As the listing requirements for the Tokyo Stock Exchange and Jasdaq have loosened, so has the flow of private equity dollars. Listed companies are no longer required to have three years of consistent earnings to launch an IPO, thereby increasing the chances of venture investment liquidation.

According to a study by *Venture Economics*, a record ¥164bn ($1.34bn) was raised in 48 funds in the first half of 2000, compared to ¥134.7bn raised in all of 1999. The *Nihon Keizai Shimbum* reported that venture capital disbursements reached ¥420.1bn in fiscal 2000 (March), compared to ¥299bn in 1999, a record year. Further, the number of active venture funds in Japan rose 23% to 160 in 2000 from 130 in 1996 (*VCJ*, January 2001). The Japanese, however, have not eluded the fallout in the dotcom marketplace. *Venture Economics* reports that disbursements in the first half of 2001 fell to $405mn, compared to $1.3bn in the first half of 2000.

Whether or not Mr. Hiranuma's goal of 1000 venture firms in three years will be achieved, Japan's venture marketplace has taken marked steps toward a more "laissez-faire" environment and, as such, has attracted more institutional funds than at any time in its history.

LATIN AMERICA

Not far behind the private equity boom of Europe and Asia stands Latin America. Despite some of the crises Latin America has gone through in the 90s, it has still experienced substantial expansion. Growth figures can be largely attributed to privatizations of formerly government-regulated industries. Private equity firms have taken notice. *Venture Capital Journal* reports that an estimated $1.9bn was raised in new funds in 2000, down from $3.6bn in 1998, but more than 1999"s $804mn.

At the third annual conference on Latin American private equity, private equity firms were asked where the geographic focus would be over the next couple of years. The response indicated that 60% would focus on Brazil, and 37% toward Mexico, and 3% toward Argentina (*VCJ*, March 2001).

Brazil

Brazil is the overwhelming favorite of private equity firms because of an improving macroeconomic situation and continuously decreasing interest rates. The *Index of Economic Freedom* reports that:

> "seasonably adjusted GDP growth of 1.2 per cent for the first quarter 2000 and inflation under control."
>
> *VCJ, February 2001*

Private equity activity in Brazil reached record highs in 2000, announcing 87 deals, a 129% increase over 1999. However, Brazil has its issues. H.M. Werner of *Venture Capital Journal*, says:

> "In Brazil, substantial barriers remain to foreign investment. Foreigners may not own or run media, broadcasting, airlines, some real estate, lotteries, atomic power or alternative energy."
>
> *VCJ, February 2001*

Further, Brazil continues to struggle with its tax and social security systems.

Alvaro Gonzalvez, a partner at Stratus Invesimentos Ltda., had this to say about the near term private equity outlook in Brazil:

> "Two factors should be closely monitored going forward in assessing the scenario for private equity in Brazil in [2001]. These are the increasing presence of players not affiliated with financial institutions and the tendency toward small to medium-sized investments. These [small to medium-sized investments] will replace the privatizations in 1997-1998 and the pure Internet plays in 1999-2000".
>
> *VCJ, March 2001*

Mexico

As for Mexico, Luis Porras, principal of Monterrey Capital Partners, believes that the time is right for private equity.

"There is an abundance of SMEs (small to medium enterprises) that are undercapitalized. There is a scarcity of professional management. Business opportunities have been generated by NAFTA and now with Europe. And family-owned companies are facing a third generation change."

VCJ, March 2001

Private equity development however, has been slow. Despite a NAFTA-driven 7% growth rate in 2000, the struggle to overcome the country's family-owned business climate has been difficult. *Venture Capital Journal* reports that:

"private equity capital in Mexico is lower than either Brazil or Argentina."

VCJ, March 2001

Despite its issues, Mexico's biggest private equity players since 1992 represent some of the industry's top firms, including, Hicks, Muse Tate & Furst, J.P. Morgan Capital Corporation, CVC Latin America and the Blackstone Group, Newbridge Latin America, and Advent International. Investments have been diverse with 19% in telecommunications, 17% in food and beverage, 15% in financial services, 13% in media and entertainment, 9% in retail, 5% in construction, 1% in information technology, and 21% in other sectors (*VCJ*, March 2001).

As private equity continues to expand in Mexico, the Mexican congress is faced with decisions on important fiscal reforms designed to promote private and foreign investment. The government's ability to adjust will play an important role in the continued evolvement of private equity culture.

MIDDLE EAST: ISRAEL

Israel has recognized a significant growth in its venture capital market over the past decade. The growth, in part, was spawned through the efforts of the Israeli Defense Force following the Six Day War in 1967. The Defense Force, following a decision by the French government to limit the supply of military technology, was forced to instigate its independence efforts through entrepreneurial development in the defense related sector (*Venture Capital Journal*, July 2001).

"When the government itself began incubating high-tech startups in 1991, the Israel Defense Force already had created a generation of entrepreneurs through elite intelligence units specializing in network security and Internet support systems."

VCJ, July 2001

The efforts of the Israeli government to ignite technological independence have attracted attention from some of the world's largest private equity institutions.

Before 1999, venture capital activity was almost non-existent in Israel. *Venture Capital Journal* reports that by 1999, private equity investments reached $1bn, and by 2000, the figure had climbed to $3bn. And while recent activity has declined, some very powerful American venture capital firms have come onto the Israeli landscape to take advantage of the high-tech atmosphere.

Benchmark Capital announced in early May 2001 that it had closed on a $220mn fund focused on early-stage Israeli high-tech companies. Sequoia Capital, another private equity mammoth, announced its first Israeli fund in March 2001, which closed at $150mn (*The Industry Standard*, May 7, 2001).

Benchmark operating partner Steve Spurlock comments:

"Israel is often referred to as the 51st [US] state by people in the business. The infrastructure mirrors the US closely."

The Industry Standard, May 7, 2001

Dr Avishai Braverman, president of Ben-Gurion University of the Negev in Be'er Sheva, says:

"Israel still remains the place for knowledge capital in high-tech, biotech and medical technology."

VCJ, July 2001

The Middle East has its drawbacks. Israel endures a highly volatile political climate. Investors, however, have found the potential rewards worth the risk. Harvey Krueger, Lehman Brothers' vice chairman, says:

> "People may be afraid to come to Israel, but investors have no choice. If they want to invest in high-tech, they'll invest in Israel."
> *The Industry Standard, March 26, 2001*

Benchmark's Spurlock adds:

> "The political conflict doesn't have a lot of impact in the Tel Aviv area, which is where most high-tech companies are located, on a day-to-day basis."
> *The Industry Standard, May 7, 2001*

While the appetite for Israeli companies has slowed in recent months, the arrival of highly respected private equity institutions, combined with the fact that Israel was third, behind the United States and Canada, in Nasdaq listings in 2000, points toward a healthy private equity climate going forward, despite the political unrest.

AUSTRALIA

The Australian venture capital market, like many across the globe, has reached a record high in recent years, and the sentiment is that only the tip of the iceberg has been chipped. Allen Aaron, general partner at Technology Venture Partners, says:

> "The Australian market never reached quite the buoyant heights as the US market, and it was never as over-hyped. [Our] public markets have remained fairly stable. We are also in the fortunate position here to learn from the experience of investors in the US markets. We didn't have the same degree [of fallout] and have had much fewer casualties."
> *VCJ, June 2001*

The Australian government has contributed, at least partially, to the favorable venture climate. A number of regulatory reforms were passed in recent years, including a capital gains tax reform, and roll-over relief and zero taxation for United States and other pension funds. The results speak for themselves. According to *Venture Economics* and the Australian Venture Capital Association, venture capitalists raised a record A$1.2bn and disbursed A$831mn in fiscal 2000 (June 30). In addition, a record high 42 funds were raised in 2000, nearly double the number in 1999. Stuart Wardman-Browne, chief operating officer of AMWIN Management had this to say:

> "I think 2000 was a landmark year because it achieved, not necessarily critical mass, but the first stage of critical mass."
>
> *VCJ, June 2001*

Whether or not the Australian market will be affected by the recent fallout of the United States market remains to be seen. The arrival of top-tier firms, such as J.P. Morgan Chase, ABN AMRO, and Ericsson Deutsche Technology Fund, in addition to the country's more favorable venture climate, leads one to believe the outlook down under is favorable.

RESOURCES

Venture Capital Journal, January 1, 2001, "Invest in Japan Now, Despite Problems," say VCs, Barbara Etzel.

The Industry Standard, May 7, 2001, "Benchmark to Invest $220 Million in Israeli Startups," Lark Park.

The Industry Standard, March 26, 2001, "Embattled Israel Is Still a Promising Land," Ziv Navoth.

Venture Capital Journal, July 2001, "Despite Slowdown and Violence, Israeli VC Market Remains Confident," Carolina Braunschweig.

Venture Capital Journal, March 1, 2001, "A New Year, A New Latin American Strategy," edited by Holly Werner.

Venture Capital Journal, February 2001, "Investors Remain Bullish on Latin America Despite Quiet Year," H.M. Werner.

Venture Capital Journal, July 2001, "Despite Slowdown and Violence, Israeli VC Market Remains Confident," Carolina Braunschweig.

Venture Capital Journal, September 2001, "Market at Crossroads: VCs Navigate Uncertain Path to Profitability", Jennifer Strauss.

Venture Capital Journal, September 2001, "As Deregulation Efforts Continue in Japan, Foreign VCs Impact Industry," Sherwin Yoon.

Venture Capital Journal, August 2001, "Staying Afloat: VCs Raise Annex Funds to Buoy Waning Portfolios," Carolina Braunschweig.

Venture Capital Journal, June 2001, "With Companies Faltering, VCs Look at Redemption Exit," Charles R. Fellers.

Venture Capital Journal, June 2001, "Despite Downturn, Australian VC Industry is Poised to Reach Critical Mass," Sherwin Yoon.

Venture Capital Journal, May 2001, "No More Easy Street: VCs Tighten the Purse Strings," Carolina Braunschweig.

Venture Capital Journal, May 2001, "Making an Exit: VCs Examine their Options," Charles R. Fellers.

Venture Capital Journal Supplement, September 2001, "Private Equity in Europe, Despite Economic Slowdown, European Private Equity Looks Healthy," Ken Ryan.

Venture Capital Journal Supplement, September 2001, "Private Equity in Europe, Is Europe's Venture Capital Market Finally Emerging From the Hotbed?," Andre P. Jaeggi.

Venture Capital Journal Supplement, September 2001, "Private Equity in Europe, Institutional Investors Get Back In The Driver's Seat," Lisa Bushrod.

Venture Capital Journal Supplement, September 2001, "Private Equity in Europe, Searching for Exits: VCs Hope for Better Days Amid Drought Conditions," Alistair Christopher.

Venture Capital Journal Supplement, September 2001, "Private Equity in Europe, Technology Continues to Drive European Venture Investing," Daniel Primrack.

Venture Capital Journal Supplement, September 2001, "Private Equity in Europe, US Private Equity Firms See Europe as Region of Opportunity," Leslie Green.

The Industry Standard, January 29, 2001, "VCs Thrill Ride Takes Sharp Plunge," Lark Park.

Money Tree Survey Q2 2001 Results, Tracy T. Lefteroff, Kirk Walden, PricewaterhouseCoopers.

Venture Capital Journal, February 2001, "2000 is Positive, But Not as Good as 1999," Charles Fellers.

The Industry Standard, February 7, 2001, "2000 Was a Record Year For Venture Capital, But . . .," Vishesh Kumar.

Experienced Venture Firms Continue to Raise Impressive Levels of Capital: Industry Stays Committed to Early Stage Investing, August 31, 2001, National Venture Capital Association Website (www.nvca.com).

Glossary

This chapter provides a detailed A-Z glossary on the topic and the terms associated with all aspects of angel capital.

AN A-Z GLOSSARY ANGEL FINANCING TERMS

Acquisition/merger – A combination of two or more entities into one. The most common exit for venture investors.

Angel club – An organization of angel investors designed to streamline the process of early-stage angel investing.

Angel investor – A wealthy individual who invests in seed or early-stage entrepreneurial companies.

Anti-dilution – A provision undertaken by private equity investors to maintain their existing equity ownership in a portfolio company.

Asset – Anything owned that has marketable value.

Authorized shares – A number of shares of each category of stock a corporation can issue according to its charter.

Automatic conversion – The automatic conversion of an investor's preferred position in a company prior to an initial public offering.

Balance sheet – A financial statement detailing a company's assets, liabilities, and equity.

Board of directors – An assembly of advisors typically sought after by early-stage companies seeking business advice as well as credibility. Many private equity investors utilize a seat on the board of directors of investee companies as a lever to influence the direction of the portfolio company.

Boilerplate – A term used to describe standard wording in contracts and other business documents.

Bootstrapping – Efforts taken by capital seeking entrepreneurs to finance a venture without the participation of traditional sources of capital.

Boutique – A small, typically regional investment bank with a specific financial service function.

Bridge financing – A round of financing used to carry a company from one financing event to the next.

Burn rate – A term used to describe the amount of money being spent on a monthly basis by an enterprise losing money.

Business plan – A documented summary of a business used to guide the company as well as to attract financial investors.

Capital – Ownership equity in a business.

Capital gain – Positive return on investment equal to the amount returned less the principal amount of the investment.

Capital loss – Negative return on investment equal to the principal amount invested less the amount returned.

Capital stock – The aggregate of a corporation's stock, including common and preferred stock.

Cash flows – A measure of the cash flowing in and out of a business.

Common stock – The basic unit of the corporation, the simplest form of equity security.

Convertible equity or debt – A security that can be converted into another security of the company typically common stock.

Corporation – A legal entity whereby the entity's owners are separate from the entity itself.

Deal flow – Describes a flow of investment opportunities.

Debenture – An interest-bearing debt instrument issued against the full faith and credit of a corporation with no specific pledge of assets.

Default – Describes the failure of a borrower to honor terms set forth in agreement.

Dilution – A reduction in the percentage ownership interests of the existing shareholders of an enterprise.

Due diligence – A process of investigation by investors of investment opportunities, including the analysis of management, product, market, investment terms, etc.

Elevator pitch – Generally describes an entrepreneur's summation of an investment opportunity in a very short period of time.

Enterprise – A business undertaking or venture.

Entrepreneur – An individual with an enterprising outlook toward capitalism.

Equity – The residual interest in the assets of an entity that remains after liabilities are accounted for.

Exit – Generally describes the liquidation of an investment strategy or liquidity event.

Exit strategy – Generally describes the entrepreneur's planned exit of the company. A critical component of evaluating any venture.

Expenses – Outflows of cash or the use of other assets for the purpose of operating an enterprise.

Financial statements – Reports of a company stating its financial position.

Finder – Financial intermediary acting as a "middle-man" between entrepreneurs seeking capital and the investors who hold it.

Full ratchet – A provision employed by private equity investors to protect themselves from dilution by contracting for a full downward adjustment of the conversion price of their preferred stock to match that of a subsequent issuance of stock if it happens to be issued at a lower price.

Future value – The suggested amount an investment will be worth in the future assuming a compounded rate of return.

General partner – A partner in a limited partnership generally responsible for the day-to-day operations of the partnership.

Holding period – References a period of time when an investor's investment is illiquid.

Intellectual property – An idea that can be protected legally by copyright, patent, or trademark.

Internal rate of return (IRR) – The discount rate that positions net present value at zero.

Investee firm – The company receiving an investment of capital.

Investment advisor – A financial intermediary typically focused on providing investment advice to individuals and/or organizations involved in the financial markets.

Investment bank – A financial intermediary involved in any number of activities associated with servicing the individuals and organizations involved in the financial markets.

Initial public offering (IPO) – The sale of a company's shares to the investing public for the first time.

Lead investor – The first investor in a venture. Typically lead investors are responsible for setting the terms of investment for follow-on investors.

Leveraged buyout (LBO) – A financial transaction whereby an investor, or group of investors acquires an entity using borrowed funds secured by the assets of the entity being acquired.

Liabilities – Future sacrifices of an enterprise.

Limited partner – An investor in a limited partnership. Limited partners play a passive role in the everyday operations of the partnership.

Limited partnership – An organized entity governed by a partnership agreement; the most popular organizational structure of private equity funds.

Liquidation – Generally describes the selling of the assets of a business.

Lone angels – Angel investors typically managing their own early-stage investing affairs. Typically, deeply rooted, successful professional investors.

Management fee – A fee earned by private equity firms for the management of a portfolio of assets.

Mezzanine – Commonly describes a round of venture financing; typically structured as a subordinated debt transaction with some level of continued upside through warrants.

Monitoring – The practice of nurturing a portfolio company to a successful exit

Net asset value – The measured value of a private equity fund's holdings.

Net present value – The expected value of a future stream of cash flows discounted to present time utilizing a discount factor commensurate with the risk of the venture's projections.

Options – The right, but not the obligation, to buy or sell a security at a fixed price over a fixed period of time.

Participating preferred stock – Preferred stock that positions its holders to receive additional dividends with common stockholders.

Placement agent – A financial intermediary whose services are employed by those seeking capital (i.e. entrepreneurs and private equity firms).

Portfolio company – A company invested in by a private equity investor.

Post-money valuation – The value of an enterprise following a financing round.

Preferred stock – Stock of entity that has preferences over common stock in terms of dividends, liquidation, etc.

Pre-money valuation – The value of an enterprise prior to a financing round.

Present value – Today's value of a future stream of cash flows discounted at an interest rate commensurate with the risk of the cash flows.

Price-earnings ratio – The market price of a company's common stock divided by its earnings per share.

Private equity firms – Financial organizations typically focused on venture capital, leveraged buyouts, or mezzanine financing.

Risk capital – Assets invested in high-risk ventures.

Restricted stock – Stock of a company that is restricted from being sold under certain conditions at certain points in time.

Return on investment (ROI) – The return per dollar of investment.

Road show – The marketing of venture to potential investors in a number of different locations.

Screening – The process of evaluating ventures for potential investment. Screening naturally takes place before due diligence.

Seed stage – An idea; a venture in the process of organization.

Small business investment company (SBIC) – A pool of capital guaranteed by the federal government.

Start-up – A venture in the early stages of product development; typically less than two years old.

Stockholders equity – The owner's equity of a corporation.

Sweat equity – A term used by entrepreneurs to describe the amount of time and effort invested in building a company.

Syndication – An organized group of investors or intermediaries joining forces to complete the financing of a venture.

Time value of money – The concept that future cash flows have less value than cash flows of today.

Tombstone – An advertisement used to announce a financing.

Treasury stock – Shares of a corporation re-acquired by the issuing corporation.

Valuation – A financial measure undertaken to determine the value of an enterprise prior to making an investment decision.

Venture capital – Managed funds dedicated to the purpose of equity based financings in high-growth companies.

Venture capitalist – A member of the general partner of venture capital fund.

Warrant – An option to buy stock of a company at a fixed price over a fixed period of time.

Yield – The interest rate of return on a stream of cash flows.

Resources

This chapter lists practitioners, books, articles, and useful Websites on the topic.

PRIVATE EQUITY EVENT DIRECTORY

» *Event*: Alley to the Valley 2000 Conference;
  Website: www.alleyvalley.com
» *Event*: Annual Conference for Private and Institutional Investors;
  Website: www.CapitalMissions.com
» *Event*: Arizona Venture Capital Conference (AVCC);
  Website: www.phoenixchamber.com/avcc
» *Event*: A.S.A.P. E-Business Alliance Summit;
  Website: www.strategic-alliances.org
» *Event*: Barbarians on the Net Conference presented by Strategic
  Research Institute's Private Equity Group;
  Website: www.srinstitute.com
» *Event*: California Venture Forum;
  Website: www.calventureforum.org
» *Event*: Central Coast Venture Forum; *Website*: www.ccvf.org
» *Event*: CEO Global Breakfast Series; *Website*: www.scu.edu
» *Event*: Corporate Investment & Strategic Alliance Conference;
  Website: www.tccic.org
» *Event*: Corporate Venturing and Strategic Investing;
  Website: www.ibforum.com
» *Event*: DealQuest Private Equity Markets Summit;
  Website: www.iir-ny.com
» *Event*: Diamond Venture Forum;
  Website: www.diamondventure.com
» *Event*: Emerging Technology Business Showcase;
  Website: www.edc-tech.org
» *Event*: Entrepreneurship Capital Conference;
  Website: www.uclaextension.org
» *Event*: Family Office Forum; *Website*: www.iir-ny.com
» *Event*: Fund of Funds; *Website*: www.iir-ny.com
» *Event*: Global Alternative Investment Management Forum (GAIM);
  Website: www.icbi-uk.com/gaim/
» *Event*: Illinois Venture Capital Conference;
  Website: www.ventureconference.com

» *Event*: International Energy Project Financing Conference;
Website: www.energy.ca.gov/export

» *Event*: Massachusetts Software Council Investment Conference;
Website: www.swcouncil.org

» *Event*: Marin Technology Venture Forum;
Website: www.marinventure.com

» *Event*: Mergers, Acquisitions, and Business Valuation Seminar;
Website: www.nccetraining.com

» *Event*: The Natural Business Financial, Investment and Market Trends
Conference for Natural, Organic and Nutritional Products;
Website: www.naturalbusiness.com

» *Event*: New Jersey Venture Fair; *Website*: www.njventurefair.njtc.org

» *Event*: New York City Venture Capital Conference and Exposition;
Website: www.nycvc.com

» *Event*: Northeast Venture Conference;
Website: www.northeastvc.com

» *Event*: The Private Equity Analyst Conference;
Website: www.assetnews.com

» *Event*: Private Equity in Transition Conference;
Website: www.srinstitute.com

» *Event*: Private Investment Strategies Summit;
Website: www.iir-ny.com

» *Event*: Southern California Technology Venture Forum;
Website: www.laedc.org/sctvfmain/html

» *Event*: Springboard 2000 Women's Venture Capital Forum;
Website: www.springboard2000.org

» *Event*: Tax, Accounting and Documentation Requirements for Private
Investment Ownerships Seminar; *Website*: www.iir-ny.com

» *Event*: Tax Advantaged Investment and Planning strategies to Opti-
mize Wealth Forum; *Website*: www.irr-ny.com

» *Event*: Venture Capital Financing Conference;
Website: www.cle.com

» *Event*: Venture Forum, publishers of *Venture Capital Journal*;
Website: www.tfn.com

» *Event*: VentureNet; *Website*: www.venturenet.org

VENTURE NETWORKS

Arizona

» *Group*: Arizona Technology Incubator; *location*: Scottsdale, Arizona; *Website*: www.asu.edu/ia/economic/ati

California

» *Group*: Angel Strategies, LLC; *location*: Aliso Viejo, California; *Website*: www.angelstrategies.com
» *Group*: Cal Tech/MIT Enterprise Forum; *location*: Pasadena, California; *Website*: www.caltech.edu/-entforum
» *Group*: Garage Technology Ventures; *location*: Palo Alto, California; *Website*: www.garage.com
» *Group*: Los Angeles Venture Association; *location*: Santa Monica, California; *Website*: www.lava.org
» *Group*: Orange County Venture Group; *location*: Laguna hills, California; *Website*: www.ocvg.org
» *Group*: UCSD Connect; *location*: La Jolla, California; *Website*: www.connect.org

Colorado

» *Group*: Ctech Angels; *location*: Denver, Colorado; *Website*: www.wjbradley.com
» *Group*: W.J. Bradley Company; *location*: Denver, Colorado; *Website*: www.wjbradley.com
» *Group*: The Rockies Venture Club; *location*: Denver, Colorado; *Website*: www.rockiesventureclub.org

Connecticut

» *Group*: Connecticut Venture Group; *location*: Fayetteville, Connecticut; *Website*: www.ct-ventures.org

Florida

» *Group*: North Florida Venture Capital Network; *location*: Jacksonville, Florida; *Website*: www.enfc.org
» *Group*: The Central Florida Innovation Corporation; *location*: Orlando, Florida; *Website*: www.cfic.org

Georgia

» *Group*: Merritt Capital Services; *location*: Rosewell, Georgia; *Website*: www.merrittcap.com

Idaho

» *Group*: Rocky Mountain Venture Group; *location*: Idaho Falls, Idaho; *Website*: www.rmyg.org

Indiana

» *Group*: Private Investors Network; *location*: Bloomington, Indiana *Website*: www.thestarcenter.com
» *Group*: Indiana Business Modernization and Technology Corporation; *location*: Indianapolis, Indiana; *Website*: www.bmtadvantage.org
» *Group*: Venture Club of Indiana; *location*: Indianapolis, Indiana; *Website*: www.ventureclub.org

Iowa

» *Group*: Venture Network of Iowa; *location*: Des Moines, Iowa; *Website*: www.state.ia.us/sbro

Kansas

» *Group*: Kansas Technology Enterprise Corporation; *location*: Topeka, Kansas; *Website*: www.ktec.com

Kentucky

» *Group*: The Venture Club of Louisville; *location*: Louisville, Kentucky; *Website*: www.ventureclub-louisville.org

Maine

» *Group*: Maine Investment Exchange; *location*: Portland, Maine; *Website*: www.mixforum.org

Maryland

» *Group*: Baltimore Washington Venture Group; *location*: College Park, Maryland; *Website*: www.mbs.umd.edu

Massachusetts

» *Group*: 128 Venture Capital Group; *location*: Lincoln, Massachusetts; *Website*: www.erols.com/vcg
» *Group*: Technology Capital Network at MIT; *location*: Cambridge, Massachusetts; *Website*: www.tenmit.org

» *Group*: Startup Group; *location*: Boston, Massachusetts; *Website*: www.sug1.com

Michigan

» *Group*: Environmental Capital Network; *location*: Ann Arbor, Michigan; *Website*: www.bizserve.com/ecn
» *Group*: Southeastern Michigan Venture Group; *location*: Grosse Pointe, Michigan; *Website*: www.semug.com

Minnesota

» *Group*: Coral Ventures; *location*: Minneapolis, Minnesota; *Website*: www.coralventures.com
» *Group*: The Collaborative; *location*: Minneapolis, Minnesota; *Website*: www.collaborative-online.com
» *Group*: Minnesota Investment Network; *location*: Minneapolis, Minnesota; *Website*: www.mincorp.org

Montana

» *Group*: Montana Private Capital Network; *location*: Polson, Montana; *Website*: www.mbc.umt.edu

New Hampshire

» *Group*: The Breakfast Club; *location*: Milford, New Hampshire; *Website*: www.barn.org
» *Group*: New Hampshire Business Development Corporation; *location*: Manchester, New Hampshire; *Website*: www.nhbdc.com

New Jersey

» *Group*: New Jersey Entrepreneurial Network; *location*: Princeton, New Jersey; *Website*: www.njen.com
» *Group*: New Jersey Technology Council; *location*: Princeton, New Jersey; *Website*: www.njtc.org
» *Group*: Venture Association of New Jersey; *location*: Morristown, New Jersey; *Website*: www.vanj.com

North Carolina

» *Group*: U.S. Investor Network; *location*: Raleigh, North Carolina; *Website*: www.usinvestor.com

Ohio
» *Group*: National Business Incubation Association; *location*: Athens, Ohio; *Website*: www.nbia.org

Oregon
» *Group*: Oregon Entrepreneurs Forum; *location*: Portland, Oregon; *Website*: www.oef.org

Pennsylvania
» *Group*: Pennsylvania Private Investors Group; *location*: Philadelphia, Pennsylvania; *Website*: www.ppig.com
» *Group*: Ben Franklin Technology Center of Southeastern Pennsylvania; *location*: Philadelphia, Pennsylvania; *Website*: www.benfranklin.org

Rhode Island
» *Group*: Brown University Research Foundation; *location*: Providence, Rhode Island; *Website*: www.brown.edu

South Carolina
» *Group*: Private Investors Network; *location*: Aiken, South Carolina; *Website*: www.gabn.net
» *Group*: The South Carolina Technology Alliance; *location*: Columbia, South Carolina; *Website*: www.sctech.org

Texas
» *Group*: MIT Enterprise Forum of Texas, Inc.; *location*: Houston, Texas; *Website*: www.miteftx.com
» *Group*: MIT Enterprise Forum of Dallas-Fort Worth, Inc.; *location*: Dallas, Texas; *Website*: www.flash.net
» *Group*: Southwest Venture Forum; *location*: Dallas, Texas; *Website*: www.smu.edu

Utah
» *Group*: Wayne Brown Institute; *location*: Salt Lake City, Utah; *Website*: www.venturecapital.org

Vermont
» *Group*: Vermont Investor's Forum; *location*: Waterbury, Vermont; *Website*: www.gmtcap.com/vif

» *Group*: Vermont Venture Network; *location*: Burlington, Vermont; *Website*: www.vermontventurenetwork.com
» *Group*: Vermont Investor's Forum; *location*: Waterbury, Vermont; *Website*: www.gmtcap.com/vif

Virginia

» *Group*: Hampton Roads Private Investors Network; *location*: Chesapeake, Virginia; *Website*: www.hrccva.com
» *Group*: The Dinner Club; *location*: Vienna, Virginia; *Website*: www.thedinnerclub.com

Washington

» *Group*: Northwest Capital Network; *location*: Seattle, Washington; *Website*: www.nwcapital.org
» *Group*: Wisconsin Venture Network; *location*: Milwaukee, Wisconsin; *Website*: www.maxnetwork.com/wvn

INTERNET DIRECTORY

» *Web host*: Angel Strategies, LLC; *Website*: www.angelstrategies.com
» *Web host*: Garage Technology Ventures; *Website*: http://www.garage.com
» *Web host*: International Capital Resources (ICR); *Website*: http://www.icrnet.com
» *Web host*: Off-Road Capital; *Website*: http://www.offroadcapital.com
» *Web host*: W.J. Bradley Company; *Website*: www.wjbradley.com

SUGGESTED READING LIST

Venture Capital Journal, "Invest in Japan Now, Despite Problems, say VCs," by Barbara Etzel, January 1, 2001

The Industry Standard, May 7, 2001, "Benchmark to Invest $220 Million in Israeli Startups," Lark Park.

The Industry Standard, March 26, 2001, "Embattled Israel Is Still a Promising Land," Ziv Navoth.

Venture Capital Journal, July 2001, "Despite Slowdown and Violence, Israeli VC Market Remains Confident," Carolina Braunschweig.

Venture Capital Journal, March 1, 2001, "A New Year, A New Latin American Strategy," edited by Holly Werner.

Venture Capital Journal, February 2001, "Investors Remain Bullish on Latin America Despite Quiet Year," H.M. Werner.

Venture Capital Journal, September 2001, "Market at Crossroads: VCs Navigate Uncertain Path to Profitability," Jennifer Strauss.

Venture Capital Journal, September 2001, "As Deregulation Efforts Continue in Japan, Foreign VCs Impact Industry," Sherwin Yoon.

Venture Capital Journal, August 2001, "Staying Afloat: VCs Raise Annex Funds to Buoy Waning Portfolios," Carolina Braunschweig.

Venture Capital Journal, June 2001, "With Companies Faltering, VCs Look at Redemption Exit," Charles R. Fellers.

Venture Capital Journal, June 2001, "Despite Downturn, Australian VC Industry is Poised to Reach Critical Mass," Sherwin Yoon.

Venture Capital Journal, May 2001, "No More Easy Street: VCs Tighten the Purse Strings," Carolina Braunschweig.

Venture Capital Journal, May 2001, "Making an Exit: VCs Examine their Options," Charles R. Fellers.

Venture Capital Journal Supplement, September 2001, "Private Equity in Europe, Despite Economic Slowdown, European Private Equity Looks Healthy," Ken Ryan.

Venture Capital Journal Supplement, September 2001, "Private Equity in Europe, Is Europe's Venture Capital Market Finally Emerging From the Hotbed?," Andre P. Jaeggi.

Venture Capital Journal Supplement, September 2001, "Private Equity in Europe, Institutional Investors Get Back In The Driver's Seat," Lisa Bushrod.

Venture Capital Journal Supplement, September 2001, "Private Equity in Europe, Searching for Exits: VCs Hope for Better Days Amid Drought Conditions," Alistair Christopher.

Venture Capital Journal Supplement, September 2001, "Private Equity in Europe, Technology Continues to Drive European Venture Investing," Daniel Primrack.

Venture Capital Journal Supplement, September 2001, "Private Equity in Europe, US Private Equity Firms See Europe as Region of Opportunity," Leslie Green.

The Industry Standard, January 29, 2001, "VCs Thrill Ride Takes Sharp Plunge," Lark Park.

The Pricewaterhouse Coopers MoneyTree Survey, Q2 2001 Results, Tracy T. Lefteroff, Kirk Walden.

Venture Capital Journal, February 2001, "2000 is Positive, But Not as Good as 1999," Charles Fellers.

The Industry Standard, February 7, 2001, "2000 Was a Record Year For Venture Capital, But . . .," Vishesh Kumar.

National Venture Capital Association Website (www.nvca.com), August 31, 2001, "Experienced Venture Firms Continue to Raise Impressive Levels of Capital Industry Stays Committed to Early Stage Investing."

The Industry Standard, June 19, 2000, "Book Review: Angel Investing: Matching Start-up Funds With Start-up Companies," Tom Ehrenfeld.

Private Equity Week, May 2, 2001, "First Quarter VC Disbursements Take A Dive," Dan Primack,

The Industry Standard, April 13, 2001, "Venture Buzz: When VC Firms Go Global", Vishesh Kumar.

The Industry Standard, November 20, 2000, "Global Funding," Lark Park.

Venture Capital Journal, July 1, 2000, "Viewpoint: Partnering Advice for Successful Overseas Ventures," Jonathan Bell.

Wealth Manager, February 2001, Bloomberg Press, page 62-.

The Angel Investor's Handbook: How to Profit From Early-Stage Investing, 2001, Gerald A. Benjamin & Joel Margulis, Bloomberg Press.

Angel Financing: How to Find and Invest in Private Equity, 2000, Gerald A. Benjamin & Joel Margulis, John Wiley & Sons.

Ten Steps to Angel Investing

This chapter presents a step-by-step guide to angel capital investing, providing the reader with an excellent framework from which to build a customized methodology.

Angel investing has proven to be more art than science. No single proven method of angel investing exists. Rather, angel investors constantly refine their processes to capitalize on the multiple returns offered by the asset class. While they find pinning down a tried-and-true method is difficult, they should be aware of several key components from which they can construct a customized process best suited to their individual needs and talents. The following ten-step process serves as a guideline for the amateur angel investor seeking a framework from which to launch a successful early-stage investing campaign.

THE TEN STEPS

1 Self-qualifying
2 Understanding
3 Planning
4 Networking
5 Formalizing
6 Evaluating
7 Investing
8 Monitoring
9 Harvesting
10 Refining

1. SELF-QUALIFYING

Goal: determine if you are fit for the challenge

Before venturing into depths of the ten steps, you must first determine whether your financial capability permits you to make investments in the risky asset class known as seed-stage private equity, or angel investing.

The "qualified" angel investor can bear the loss of their entire investment in an early-stage venture should that unfortunate circumstance befall them. Formally, the Securities and Exchange Commission, through its Rule 501 of Regulation D, defines such an individual as an "accredited investor."

Rule 501 defines an accredited investor to include "any natural person whose net worth, or joint net worth with that person's spouse, exceeds $1,000,000'' or ''any natural person who had an individual income in excess of $200,000 in each of the two most recent years, or joint income with that person's spouse in excess of $300,000 in each of those years, and has a reasonable expectation of reaching the same income level in the current year.''

If you are unable to meet the requirements set forth in Rule 501, you are not qualified to undertake investment in angel deals; your portfolio simply cannot withstand the risks. Angel investing is a high-risk game, even when you undertake that risk with the greatest caution. If you feel comfortable that you qualify as an accredited investor, and recognize that the possibility of losing your entire investment in any given venture is very real, you are ready to advance to the next step.

2. UNDERSTANDING THE BUSINESS

Goal: gain a general understanding of the business, its terms and protocol

As you have gathered from the information presented in this book, angel investing is complicated. You must obtain the knowledge of the ''who, what, when, where and why'' of angel investing to make educated investment decisions.

Too many investors, lured by the exotic potential returns of angel investing, take a blind leap, throwing hard earned dollars into poorly researched early-stage companies. It is critical that before you make any angel-stage investment, you understand the inter-weaving of the asset class.

The best way of educating yourself on any topic is through experience. So, while you must undertake efforts to capture the knowledge provided through the written word, you will learn your greatest lessons once you officially ''enter the game.'' Before coming off the bench, however, we advise you to reference '' Chapter 9 Resources '' to gather the information you need to understand the mysterious marketplaces of angel investing.

3. PLANNING

Goal: define your target

Whether you endeavor to climb a mountain, build a business, or make angel investments, establish a plan of action. The exercises associated with constructing an angel investment plan should drive you to develop, at minimum, a blueprint of the sectors you would like to target, and how many investments you would like to make given your financial risk tolerance.

What sectors you decide to target influences how you go about creating deal flow. As an amateur angel investor, you will find it to your benefit to target those sectors with which you have some familiarity. As you leverage your industry expertise, you will help yourself not only evaluate prospective deals, but provide on-going returns as you monitor and support your angel portfolio. As you gain expertise in additional industries through experience or through affiliations with fellow angels, you can branch out beyond your comfort zone. In the meantime, stick with what you know.

Once you fully digest your financial limitations – that is, once you decide the amount of capital you have to invest – you will gain a much better understanding of how to develop your angel portfolio. Once you have determined how much risk capital you have to allocate to angel investments, you must determine how many investments you would like to make over a one-, three-, and five-year period. You should expect the minimum investment in any one deal to be no less than $25,000.

Once you have determined what sectors you'd like to target and how many deals you're after, you're ready to get in game.

4. NETWORKING

Goal: develop a network of contacts within your region

To function efficiently as an angel investor, you must develop a strong network of professionals from whom you can access deal flow and expertise. First, plug into your immediate region before you attempt to expand your efforts nationally. Understanding your local climate is a critical first step to success.

Your initial networking goal is simply to establish industry contacts. Understand who the players are, and what they have to offer. Your efforts should resemble an interviewing process through which you can determine whom you want to work with.

Networking within your local community may or may not come easily to you, depending on your roots in the region. If you have a track record of success in your current location, you likely have a network of people you wish to contact. If not, identify and explore the plethora of networking organizations in every region. Your networking efforts should be focused toward four segments of the financial industry: venture capitalists, investment bankers, accountants and attorneys, and angel investors.

Breaking into the venture capital community, if you don't already have an "in," may prove to be the biggest challenge. The venture capital community is a very "clubby" group of financial professionals. As you might imagine, venture capitalists are approached everyday by people trying to poke into their pockets. As such, their guard is always up. Don't get discouraged if you fail to get in the door. You can get to where you need to go, at least initially, without the venture capitalists. Further, you will likely gain access to these institutions once you've established the other aspects of your network.

The investment banking community is an easier target, particularly the boutique shops. Investment banks are constantly developing relationships with sources of capital, and unlike venture capitalists – who don't need or want your money – investment banks recognize you as an *added* potential value. Networking with the investment banks provides an excellent opportunity for you to establish a deal flow channel, as well as gather information and insight into where you might be able to network with others like yourself.

Networking amongst the legal/accounting community should be relatively simple. You are a prospect for these professional services firms and as such, they will likely be more than willing to talk with you. These professionals are not only excellent sources of deal flow and contacts, but candidates for an essential component of due diligence team.

Uncovering angels, as mentioned throughout this book, is a difficult practice. Depending upon your location, you can probably target at least one angel organization. Further, as an angel, you should be successful in obtaining the names of fellow angels through the networking channels we previously discussed.

5. FORMALIZING THE TEAM

Goal: construct a quality network

If you've been an effective networker, formalizing your team should be a relatively easy process. Your team must be capable of providing you with two critical components of angel investing: deal flow and due diligence.

Deal flow can be sourced from each of the four groups mentioned in the networking step. The more deal flow you can generate in the beginning, the better. As such, it would be wise not to cut off sources of deal flow until you've assessed their value. Understand that you may look at one hundred deals and not find one that you like. Accept that deal flow is a numbers game, like digging for gold but finding few shining nuggets.

You must select your due diligence team with care. You will rely on when you make an angel investment. Your due diligence team should at least include an accountant and an attorney. If you've identified a quality angel club that you feel comfortable with, join it. Angel clubs are not only an excellent source of deal flow and networking, but a ready team of experts within given industries.

Boutique investment banks are another excellent consideration for your due diligence team. In addition, their services to angels should come at no cost. Deals presented to you through investment banks will be pre-screened and "investment ready." However, make every effort to leverage other members of your due diligence team when you evaluate projects presented through this channel. It never hurts to have an outside opinion from someone you trust.

6. EVALUATING

Goal: uncover quality angel investment opportunities

Entire texts are written on the evaluation of early-stage companies. The purpose of this book is not to provide you with evaluation guidelines, but to introduce you to an overview of the process.

When you evaluate early-stage companies, address at minimum the following aspects of the venture: management team, market/competition, product/service, valuation, exit strategy, and deal structure. While a detailed examination of each of the components mentioned is beyond the scope of this book, a brief capstone of each is appropriate.

» Management team: The strength of the management team (track record, experience in the industry, etc.) is often the most vital component of the venture. Examine the team in extreme detail, including background and reference checks.

» Market/competition: Is there a ready market for the venture's product/service? Can the company capture the market to the extent it has projected? Does the company have existing customers? What is the future outlook of the marketplace? What is the company's competitive advantage? Market share? As we mentioned in the planning step, you should be poised to assess the market and competition of the venture as a result of your focus on companies in industries in which you are an expert.

» Product/service: Is the product/service viable? Is the technology unique? Is it scalable? Again, your expertise in the industry should assist you in answering these questions.

» Valuation: How was the valuation determined? What are the "comparables?" What do other valuation techniques yield in comparison to that offered? Your accountant or investment banker will be able to assist you in your assessment of the company's asking price.

» Exit strategy: How will you exit your investment? Is the exit strategy realistic? Are you comfortable with the time frame to harvest? Your knowledge of the industry coupled with the expertise of your investment banker will allow you to come to terms with these questions.

» Deal structure: Is the structure of the offering conducive to investment? How will further rounds of financing have an impact on your ownership? Is the type of security offered consistent with your goals of principal protection and yield? Your attorney, accountant, and investment banker are all value-added components in answering these questions.

For a thorough uncovering of the proper tenets of evaluating early stage ventures, see the "Managing the Due Diligence" section of Benjamin & Margulis, *Angel Investor's Handbook: How to Profit From Early Stage Investing* (2001, Bloomberg Press).

7. INVESTING

Goal: make quality investments on terms you are comfortable with

Now that you and your team have properly evaluated the opportunity and determined that it is worthy of investment, you're ready to take the plunge. Unfortunately, it's not that easy.

Often, the terms offered by the entrepreneur are not consistent with what your team has in mind. As such, your team will need to present its argument and then begin negotiations. Remember, the entrepreneur needs your money, and in today's capital markets, you've got more leverage than you might think.

8. MONITORING

Goal: nurture the company to success

Congratulations, you've made your first angel investment. Nervous? You should be. The majority of early-stage companies unfortunately fail. Increasing your chances of success means that you, as a seasoned executive in the industry, must make yourself available to assist the entrepreneur in the on-going development of the company, that is, if you entertain plans for a positive harvesting event.

Monitoring your investment does not suggest that you are a watchdog, but rather a guide dog. You are now a facilitator, not a dictator. Your expertise makes you highly qualified to provide insight into the trials and tribulations often faced by your portfolio company. Further, your ability to assist the entrepreneur becomes critical to the on-going success of the enterprise in such areas as negotiating the terms of contracts, creating strategic relations, assembling a board, etc.

9. HARVESTING

Goal: multiple returns on investment

"You fail before you succeed" – or so goes the old adage. A failure, while a financial setback, can prove to be a learning experience. However, you don't need to lose to learn; after all, a winning experience may be just as valuable – and feel better too.

Harvesting can take many forms: acquisition, initial public offering, re-capitalization, earnings distribution, etc. Harvesting under certain circumstances, such as bankruptcy, may result in a negative experience, but can also generate the desired outcome. Should your evaluation, structuring, and monitoring aspects of the angel investing process be sound, you will come to know the fruitful harvest well.

10. REFINING

Goal: improve

Successful angel investing is a process. You must constantly improve your team, your evaluation processes, and your value-added monitoring capabilities. On-going networking with like-minded individuals and groups is essential to creating additional opportunities that lead to fruitful harvests.

Frequently Asked Questions (FAQs)

Q1: How does the successful angel investor access quality investment opportunities?

A: Successful angel investors recognize that uncovering a quality private market investment opportunity is a job unto itself. As such, successful angels are highly proactive in developing deal flow channels that are capable of sourcing enough deal flow to properly implement a selective investment program.

Q2: How does the successful angel investor select investment opportunities?

A: The key here is "staying close to the knitting". That is, angels that have been successful over the long term have continuously invested in private market companies from industries in which they have deep domain expertise and a history of successful involvement.

Q3: How does the successful angel investor conduct due diligence?

A: Conducting intensive due diligence is the most critical aspect of private market investing. Successful angels naturally assume the due diligence responsibility which requires that they have the expertise to manage the process themselves or they have access to a professional team able to assist their efforts.

Q4: What has the state of today's market done to private company valuations?

A: Successful angel investors understand that they can no longer accept entrepreneur driven valuation computations. The valuation analysis of comparable companies (size, stage, sector, etc.) is critical to understanding the proper pricing of a private market investment opportunity. Sources of current valuation data include PricewaterhouseCoopers' *Money Tree Survey* and *Venture Economics* VentureXpert database.

Q5: What is typical of today's investment structures from an angel's point of view?

A: Angel investors are achieving more favorable investment terms than at any time in recent memory. Angels are utilizing structuring tools such as liquidation preferences, full-ratchet provisions, and convertible preferred investments to protect themselves from potential pitfalls, while at the same time, increasing upside should the investee company execute to plan.

Q6: How does the successful angel incorporate legal counsel into the private market investment process?

A: Successful angel investors are highly efficient in negotiating deal terms on a stand-alone basis. Legal counsel is most effectively incorporated in the investment process once terms have been agreed upon.

Q7: How does the successful angel manage the monitoring of investee companies?

A: One successful angel states, ''the only time I lost my money is when I didn't have control''. Successful angels recognize the importance of being able to influence and guide the decisions of investee companies. Control is most commonly achieved through a position on the investee's board of directors.

Q8: How does the successful angel investor gain access to later stage, less risky, private market ventures?

A: The key to gaining access to later stage ventures, which require greater capital influxes, is joining co-investment syndicates. The syndicate approach promotes the both the formal and informal pooling of angel capital for positioning in larger, later stage rounds of financing.

Q9: What is the future of the angel market?

A: The angel market is experiencing tremendous growth. The overall increase in the number angels and available angel capital has launched the development of a number of structured organizations catering to the angel marketplace. Recent trends indicate that the organization of angels into both formal and informal groups has led to a more efficient marketplace.

Q10: How does one go about raising private equity from angel investors?

A: The key to raising private equity from angels is building relationships. Capital seeking entrepreneurs must endeavor to develop a strong network of institutional investors, angel investors, and financial intermediaries from which to draw interest in a private market venture. While relationships serve to create the appropriate audience, a properly documented, viable venture is a necessary prerequisite.

Index

Printed and bound in the UK by
CPI Antony Rowe, Eastbourne

Printed and bound by CPI Group (UK) Ltd, Croydon, CR0 4YY

13/04/2025

14656565-0002